Building a LOG CABIN

W. BEN. HUNT

Martino Publishing
Mansfield Centre, CT
2015

Martino Publishing
P.O. Box 373,
Mansfield Centre, CT 06250 USA

ISBN 978-1-61427-884-9

© 2015 Martino Publishing

All rights reserved. No new contribution to this publication may be reproduced, stored in a retrieval system, or transmitted, in any form or by any means, electronic, mechanical, photocopying, recording, or otherwise, without the prior permission of the Publisher.

Cover design by T. Matarazzo

Printed in the United States of America On 100% Acid-Free Paper

Building a LOG CABIN

W. BEN. HUNT

THE BRUCE PUBLISHING COMPANY
MILWAUKEE

Copyright, 1947
By W. Ben. Hunt
Printed in the United States of America

INTRODUCTION

This book is the outgrowth of the author's own experience in log-cabin construction. It was suggested by the many questions about the subject put to him the past few years by prospective builders and other interested persons. To encourage and assist such individuals this work is expressly written.

When we speak of the pioneer log cabin we commonly think of a small dwelling with a large fireplace for cooking, a puncheon or padded clay floor, etc. Built often in great haste, it had few comforts. But because the log cabin truly reflected the materials and tools and the way of life of the builders, it had genuine architectural beauty. The cabin that you are going to build will be exactly like it in many of its details.

In this book we shall be concerned primarily with the smaller type of cabin such as might be used for a summer home, a clubhouse, or perhaps a rustic home of very modest size. The more pretentious type of structure, such as the large lodge and elaborate home, is essentially similar in construction but would require detailed explanation by an experienced architect. Here fundamentals are stressed. With the methods described in the pages that follow even the inexperienced person can build himself an ordinary cabin without great trouble, if he is willing to learn how to use a saw, ax, and adz with some degree of proficiency.

The emphasis throughout is on the simplest, most practical methods that will produce the best results. The drawings show all important points and by themselves almost tell the whole story.

It is the sincere hope of the author that this work will be a real help to his fellow admirers of the heritage of which the log cabin is a part. If they derive as much pleasure and satisfaction out of building and using their own log cabin as he has, his efforts will be more than amply rewarded.

W. B. H.

CONTENTS

INTRODUCTION		5
1	The Cabin and the Site	9
2	Logs and Other Materials	16
3	Tools	19
4	Foundations and Fireplaces	22
5	Walls	30
6	Roofs	47
7	Windows, Doors, and Shutters	52
8	Floors, Stairs, and Ceilings	57
9	Partitions, Additions, and Porches	64
10	Fixtures and Fireplace Equipment	73
11	Lighting and Heating	78
12	Reconditioning Old Log Cabins	82
13	Outdoor Fireplaces	85
14	Help Wanted	92
Index		97

Chapter 1

THE CABIN AND THE SITE

The Cabin

The log cabin is a product of the woods and forest. A log cabin should appear to have grown out of the soil on which it stands. It belongs in the country and preferably near a woods. This type of structure would be absolutely out of place in the city surrounded by modern, up-to-date houses or on a skimpy, poorly selected piece of land. Properly constructed and located, the beauty of the log cabin is unique.

The simplest cabin is a one-room structure (Fig. 1). To this a porch can be added. For use as a sleeping porch or dining room during the summer months this addition can be screened and fitted with canvas drops. The porch will also serve as a convenient storage place for firewood if you plan to use your log cabin during the winter months.

Should you be in need of extra room, a lean-to kitchen such as that shown in Figure 2 built against one end will be of help. This ought to be made of logs but if necessary slabs or boards will be found satisfactory. If constructed large enough, it can be used as a bedroom.

The three-room cabin shown in Figure 3 will accommodate two to three people as a permanent dwelling. Clothes closets, cabinets, shelves, and so on will, of course, have to be added as and where needed.

Naturally the log cabins which are being erected today generally are not as primitive as those of the early settlers. Cabins are being built with some or all modern conveniences — heating, plumbing, and lighting. These features, which really require the services of architects and contractors, will be considered briefly later on.

The Site

The finest log cabin will be a failure if it is not favorably located. Hence, in selecting the site for your cabin, thoughtful consideration must be given to the following factors: drainage, water supply, orientation, accessibility, and safety. When building in the city, municipal laws, enacted to protect the citizens from danger and disease, allow no alternatives in these matters. The builder, however, usually does not encounter such rules and restrictions in rural areas. The initiative is left to you, then, to provide for the health and safety of your family and your friends.

Fig. 1. One-room cabin.

Fig. 2. One-room cabin with lean-to kitchen.

Drainage

The log cabin must be built on high solid ground. Whether you build in the woods, the mountains, along some river or lake good drainage away from the building is essential. Low land should be avoided whenever possible.

Good drainage or slope is essential to the proper functioning of the sewerage system. Septic tanks are very effective for the sanitary disposal of sewerage. Naturally, a septic tank must be lower than the house drains and at the same time cannot be set in low, wet ground because the effluent must drain off into the soil. In a properly built septic tank this effluent is crystal clear. Too often, however, the overflow is drained into a creek or river. There should be no visible overflow if the tank is correctly constructed and placed in sandy or gravel soil. An installation of this type

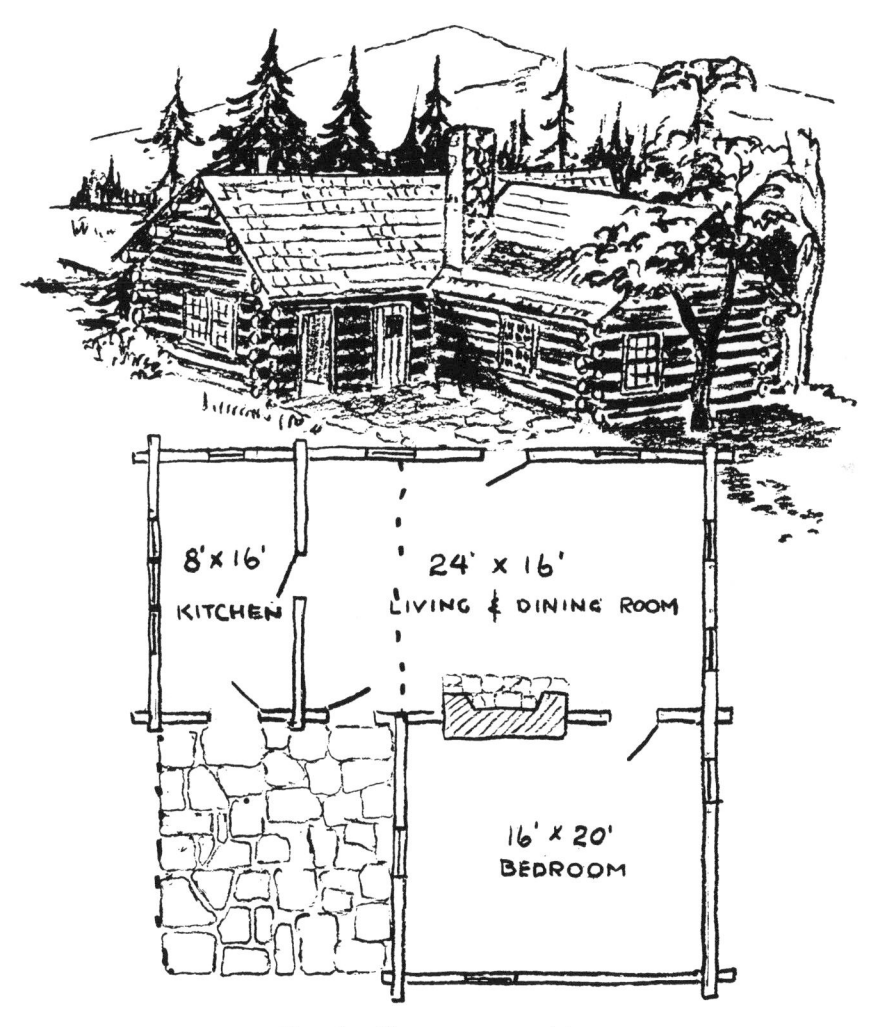

Fig. 3. Three-room cabin.

usually operates without trouble for from ten to fifteen years. After this time the tank may have to be cleaned out and new laterals may have to be dug for the overflow.

Water Supply

A clean, pure water supply must be available. In the city, water is supplied and carefully watched but in small towns and in the country it must be obtained from springs and wells.

Perhaps there is a spring on your lot. This may be your answer if there is enough of a flow. A springhouse can be erected over it and the water can be piped or pumped into the house, depending on the lay of the land. The springhouse can be used as a cooler during the summer months.

You may prefer a dug well. Dug wells are lined with stone and the water generally seeps in from the bottom because they are dug down to a level at which water is found. These wells should be covered with a tight cement or board top that has a trap door for hauling up water. A hand pump, too, can be installed.

A driven well is very satisfactory. It is made with a well point, Figure 4, which is a perforated section of pipe with a steel point at the lower end. To the upper end, sections of pipe are coupled and the point is driven into the soil. Additional sections are joined to this pipe as it is driven down until water is reached. A hand pump is used to draw the water to the surface. There are two types of points, one for ordinary and sandy soil and one for rocky soil.

Drilled wells are the best source of water supply and, of course, are more expensive than the others. They are usually termed deep wells. Gas or electric pumps can be used in connection with them. With a pumping system and a good sewerage disposal system the log cabin has some of the basic conveniences of a modern city home.

Orientation

Careful thought should be given to the direction in which the cabin is to face. The chief points to be taken into consideration are commonly designated as sunlight, prevailing winds during the various seasons, and the view.

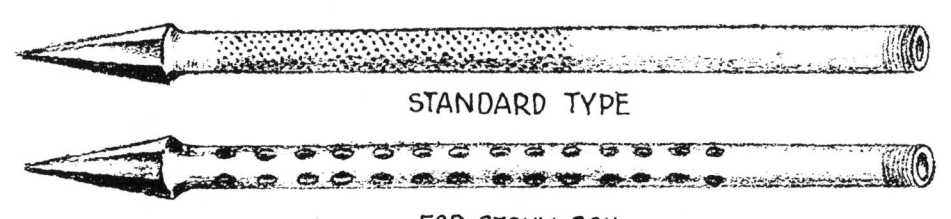

Fig. 4. Well points.

Top: Trapper's cabin in the Rockies. **Center left:** Square-hewn log cabin in the Ozarks. **Center right:** Old pioneer cabin of walnut logs in Wisconsin. **Bottom:** Mud dauber and builder in Ouachita Mountains.

[13]

Cabin of square-hewn oak logs. The author spent his boyhood days here.

In general, when you speak of view in the city the word has reference to the houses in the immediate vicinity. In the country, however, you take into consideration a different type of surrounding. You look for scenery most of all. If you are just starting out in life you can, within a few years, grow a lot of your own scenery. It takes about ten years for trees and shrubs to grow large enough to shut out a part of the landscape that may be an eyesore. With planned planting, in about twenty years you can have anything you have ever wished for. The open side of your home should be bright and cheerful and if your lot is large enough you will be able to plant so that there will be a pleasant view from every window.

It should be noted that excessive shade is not good for log cabins. The logs usually are unpainted and therefore should have a chance to dry out after rains. A cabin in a pretty shaded nook may sound and look fine, but it will become damp and uncomfortable without adequate sunlight and air. Moss in its proper place is beautiful; as far as the log cabin is concerned it does not make for human comfort.

Accessibility

It is always advantageous to build in the vicinity of a highway, especially if your cabin is to be used during the winter. However, do not get too close to a main road because of the constant rush of traffic. Side roads are fine if they are kept open. If one has to get to work on time, however, it isn't very enjoyable to have to sit and wait for the snowplow after each storm. If you are going to use your cabin during the summer months only, you need not worry about snow and sleet. For a year-round home this is an important consideration. It might not be a bad idea, then, to see your prospective site at its worst, that is, during the winter. Remember, too, that your own driveway will cause more trouble than the highway unless you plow it yourself or are able to arrange to have it plowed.

The immediate entrance to your cabin, that is, the driveway, deserves practical consideration. Money and time are required to build a driveway over low, swampy land. A hillside drive also involves a lot of bother and expense until it is packed down. If not laid correctly, the danger of washouts is always present. Moreover, such an approach can be hazardous in winter.

The proximity of churches, schools, stores, doctors, post office, bus lines, and so on, should be carefully studied in terms of your own situation.

Safety

Finally, do not overlook the safety factor in the selection of your site. Nearness of cliffs, means of escape in case of forest fire, protection from floods and storms — all of these are taken into account by the circumspect builder.

Chapter 2

LOGS AND OTHER MATERIALS

Logs

Sources of Logs

Sometimes logs can be obtained on or near the site. As a general rule, however, they will have to be procured elsewhere. Usually logs are bought from someone who has a good stand of timber. Often he will cut them and haul them for you. Sometimes they can be purchased from a saw mill or lumber company.

Kinds of Logs

You will be most fortunate if you obtain precisely what you are looking for in the way of logs. In some parts of the country obtaining them is not much of a problem, in others it is. There are cabins in Wisconsin built of logs shipped from the west coast. Sometimes a local telephone or electric power company will supply them. From a practical standpoint, electric-line poles are about the best that can be obtained as they usually are of straight, peeled cedar and have little taper.

Balsam, spruce, and white pine make excellent log cabins and are easy to work. Tamarack, if used the summer after it is cut, is also easy to work. This wood, however, is very hard when dry. Still it is often used because of its durability. The first section of my cabin was built of local tamarack. Put up some twenty-odd years ago, it still is as sound as a dollar. Poplar will last a long time if it is kept off the ground.

Although some logs naturally are easier to work than others, still, in the days when log cabins were built not so much for atmosphere as for protection from the atmosphere, the builders used whatever logs were handy. The principal requirements are that logs be straight and not have too many branches. It is difficult work to peel logs that had many branches, especially if the knots are on the inside. It is not easy to drawknife these knots and as a rule they must be chopped off smooth with an ax. It is better to use mixed logs, that is, logs of different kinds, than to use one kind if some are crooked or have too much taper.

You will also need some small logs for rafters. These are usually about half the size of the wall logs, but should be the straightest ones available.

Ordering Logs

Knowing the size of your cabin and the average size of the logs available you can determine almost to the foot how many logs you will need. By the average size of log is meant the diameter of the log at the center. Thus a log measuring 14 in. at the butt and 8 in. at the top will average 11 in. To determine the number of logs of the size required you can draw each side elevated to scale figuring the logs 11 in. in diameter the full length of the cabin. A few extra logs should be ordered, however.

Seasoning Logs

Ideally, logs should be fully dried, or seasoned, to prevent checking or cracking. There is no treatment, however, that will completely eliminate this difficulty. The logs should be peeled and then racked up so that they will not touch each other after which they are covered with hay or straw to protect them from the sun (Fig. 5). They should be allowed to stand this way for at least six months, and if possible, a year. When building is started, the inside surface of the logs should be drawknifed if they are to be oiled or stained later. This operation is performed usually as each log goes into place. It is hard work to clean the logs after they have been laid up and chinked.

Other Building Materials

While logs are the first requirement on the list of materials, other important items deserve brief consideration. You will also need sand, gravel, stone, and cement. These, of course, can be purchased from your local dealer. For your fireplace you will also have to obtain firebrick. Then there are windows, doors, roofing and flooring boards, and shingles. Your materials will also include an ample supply of oakum and plaster for chinking. Planking 2 by 6 or 2 by 8 in. will be needed for door and window frames and floor joists.

It is important that good washed sand and gravel be used for all concrete work. Be on guard against material containing dirt or clay because it will not withstand the weather. Do not line your fireplace with stone, which

Fig. 5. Logs laid out for seasoning.

may explode from the heat. Use good firebrick set in fire clay. More will be said about fireplaces later. Then, also, buy your windows before you put up the walls so that you can determine the exact width and length of the frames. Doors can be made to fit any opening if you build them yourself. If not, also buy your doors first, or you can have special doors made by a millwork company.

"As though it grew out of the soil on which it stands."

Chapter 3

TOOLS

In the pioneer days probably many log cabins were built with only an ax and a saw. Much labor and great skill certainly were required to build a good structure with such limitations. Today the worker has at his disposal a variety of high-grade tools that will make his labor simpler, more pleasant, and more effective (Fig. 6).

A 4½- or 5-ft., one- or two-man crosscut saw is indispensable, and the regular handsaw, of course, can always be used. Then you will need a hand ax. This is a very important tool and should be of good steel to keep an edge. A large ax may be useful at times but can be dispensed with, unless you wish to chop the ends of the logs. An adz is an excellent tool for hewing, but it is very dangerous in the hands of an inexperienced workman. In fact, it is dangerous at all times and must be used with caution. A broad ax will do the same work on straight cuts. However, if you have neither an adz nor a broad ax the little squaring or leveling that has to be done can be taken care of with a hand ax. You will also need a drawknife. If possible the blade should be longer than that of the ordinary drawknife. One that is used for shingles is the best for this type of work, especially if the logs are large. It will save many a bruised knuckle. Hammers you have, and if you have ever tried to drive a 60-penny spike with a claw hammer you will know that a heavier one will be a lot easier to work with. Hence, a small blacksmith's hammer is recommended. Another tool that should be mentioned, but with which few people are acquainted, is the froe (Figs. 6 and 43). This tool was formerly and most likely still is used for splitting shingles. A heavy wooden mallet is used to drive it into the wood. A large, heavy chisel and a gouge will often come in handy. The gouge should be ground on the inside, or concave, surface.

A cant hook is generally used by woodsmen for handling logs, but the author discovered that a couple of ice tongs are excellent substitutes for log-cabin construction. They are very handy for lifting and carrying logs.

You will notice the notching gauge in Figure 6. It is very effective for accurate matching. However, you will have to make it yourself. A dividers can be used as a notching gauge but it is not as accurate. Logs that are marked and cut out carefully will fit perfectly. The cut along the line is made with a large gouge and the rest of the wood is cut away with an ax or adz.

A level, plumb bob, large square, and perhaps a wrecking bar will also be

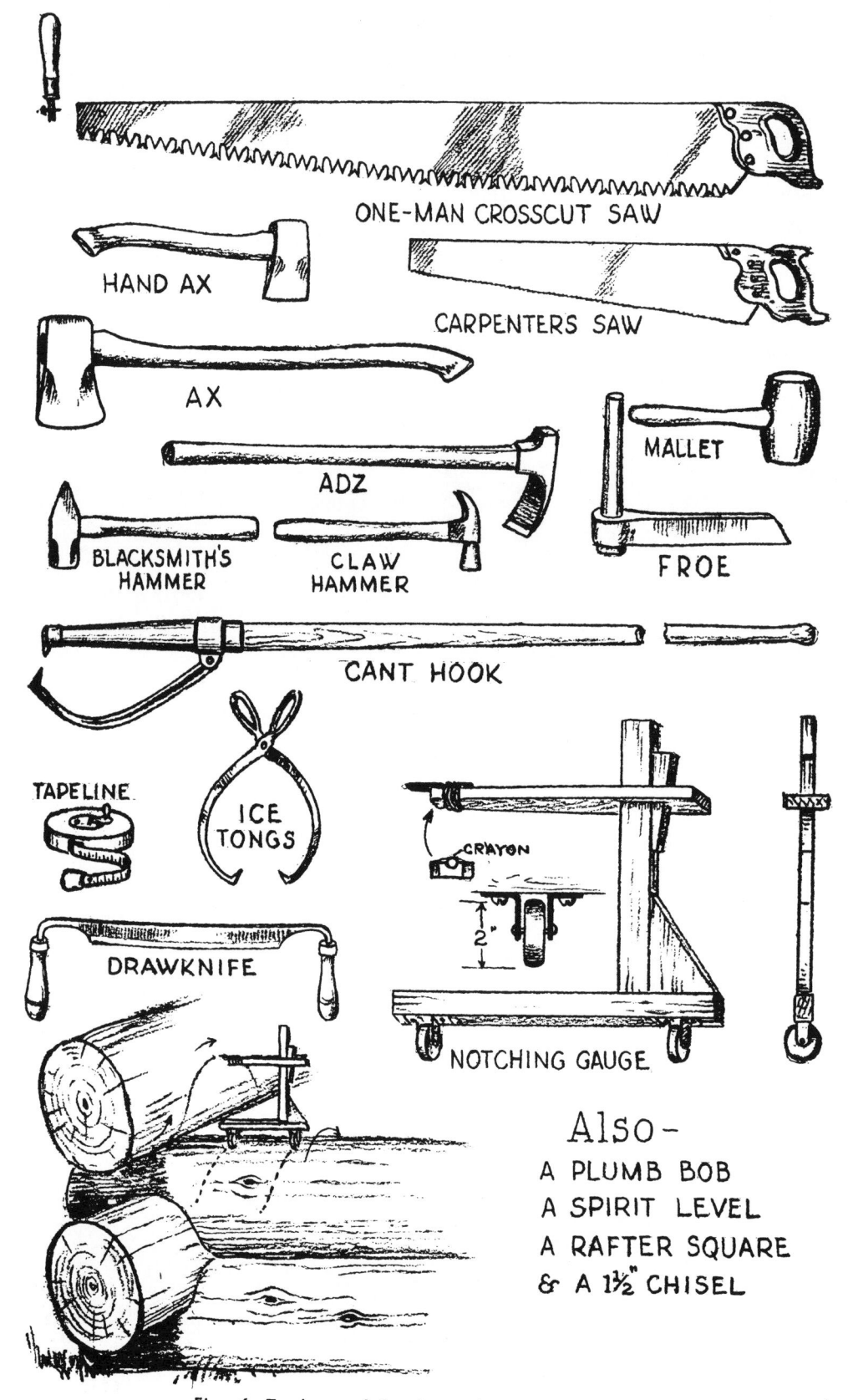

Fig. 6. Tools used for log-cabin construction.

used. The last mentioned will be found useful for pulling out spikes and prying apart logs that have to be changed (Fig. 7). A good tapeline and other rules will be required at all times. Be sure that some good black or blue marking crayon is included in your list of materials.

All tools must be sharp if you want a nice-looking cabin. Ax and drawknife cuts that show ridges and roughness present a very displeasing appearance. There is no such thing, then, as a tool that is too sharp. For this reason you should have sharpening stones handy at all times. A good grindstone will be found best for axes, adzes, chisels, and drawknives. There is no danger of burning tools and destroying their temper if they are sharpened on a grindstone. No motor is required. An emery or carborundum wheel can be used by those who are not acquainted with or who do not know how to use a grindstone, but unless such wheels are at least 6 in. in diameter there is the danger of grinding large cutting tools too hollow. A small oilstone or a whetstone will be found best for the finished edge. A couple of files — a flat-mill file and triangular file for saws — should be on hand also.

There are two ways of caring for tools. One is to go over them and hone or sharpen them before going to work each day, or to do this in the evening after work. If time is taken out to sharpen tools during working hours the progress of your helpers will be retarded. It might be a good gesture, then, to have your tools ready for use before work is begun.

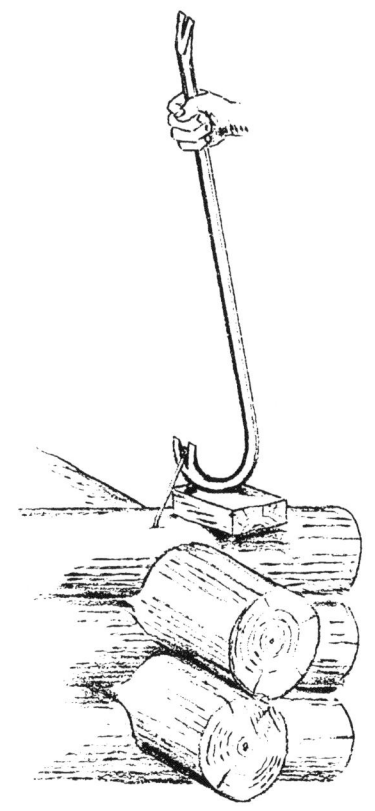

Fig. 7. Wrecking bar.

Chapter 4

FOUNDATIONS AND FIREPLACES

Preparing the Site

Whether you build on level ground or on a hillside, you will have to prepare the site. If trees must be cut down, be sure to grub out the roots especially if they will interfere with the foundation. While a cabin that is to be erected on flat land presents no particular problem at this point, a hillside house must be protected from the wash of rains. So if your tract has considerable slope, study the situation carefully and build a retaining wall or watershed as required. You will be certain then of a dry basement or, on the other hand, a dry floor.

Foundations

Three types of foundations may be distinguished: piers, foundation walls, and basements. You will probably use the first mentioned because they are easy to make and are generally quite satisfactory. For all types, a mixture of stone and concrete is recommended.

Piers

Concrete piers can be set about 6 ft. apart. They should reach down to firm ground beneath the frost line. Figure 8 shows their construction. The ground makes the form for the lower portion and a board frame for the part above the ground. A chalk line stretched level is used to determine the height. Cabins should be set low as a rule at the highest spot of the site. The tops of the piers should be only a few inches above the ground. Sometimes the piers are tapered toward the top. This is commonly done if they are set in loose soil.

A recommended mixture for concrete is 1 part of Portland cement, 2 of washed sand, and 2 to 4 of gravel. If you have never mixed concrete, it should be pointed out that dry material is easier to work than moist material. The cement must be dry. Now by a part is meant, as a general rule, a shovelful. Hence, the proportions would be 1 shovelful of cement, 2 shovelsful of sand, and so on.

Concrete can be mixed in a large or small mortar box with 6- or 8-in. sides. For small quantities a metal wheelbarrow may be practical. The ingredients are added in the following order: gravel, sand, cement. The material is then worked or mixed by shoveling back and forth until it shows an even color. Water is now added gradually until the mixture attains working consistency. It should be neither too thin nor too thick. Concrete for laying up stone should be somewhat richer. A mixture of about 1 part cement to 3 parts of sand is advisable. Rocks and stone can be used as a filler for any type of wall.

Foundation Walls and Basement

Either foundation walls or a basement, if storage space is necessary, will very likely be built if your log cabin is to be used as a permanent home. These, however, are difficult to construct so that you will do well to hire a contractor to build them for you. In the end you will be time and money ahead.

If you decide to erect a foundation wall, be sure to provide openings, 6 to 12 in. square, for ventilation. These vents are to be covered with ¼- or ½-in. screen to keep out small animals. I have been awakened more than once by a rumpus under my cabin. Usually a weasel or a mink chases a rabbit and corners him down there. They can kick up quite a fuss. The vents should be made so that they can be entirely closed during the winter.

Since bare concrete in connection with a log cabin does not present too

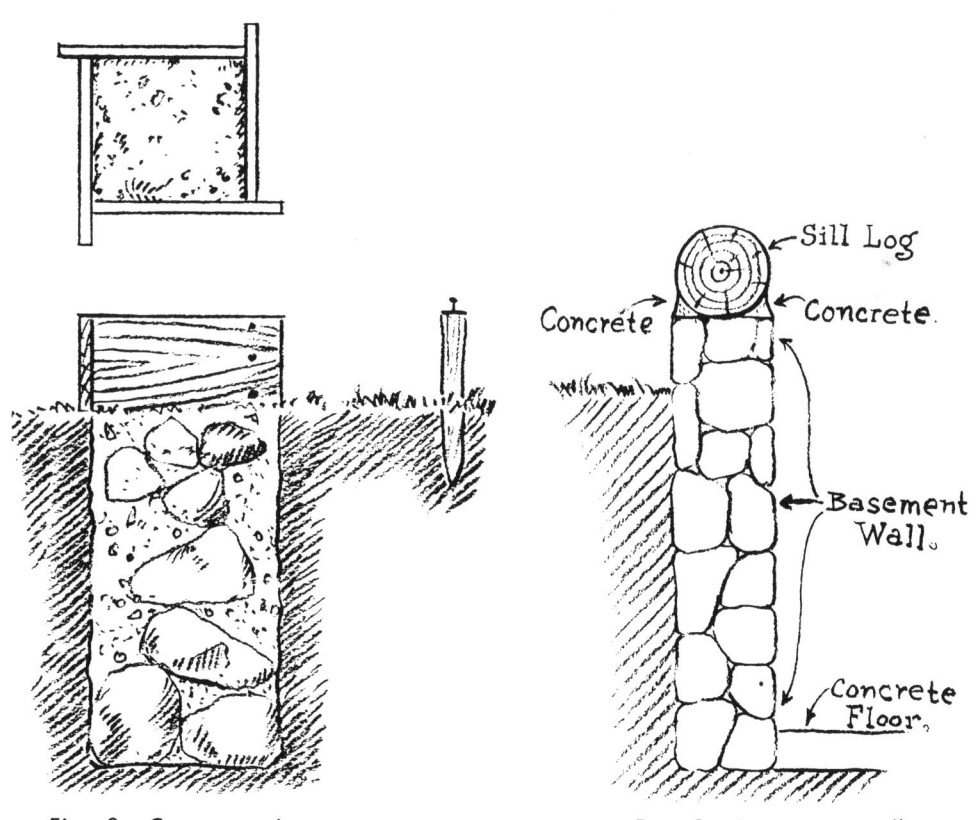

Fig. 8. Concrete pier.

Fig. 9. Basement wall.

[23]

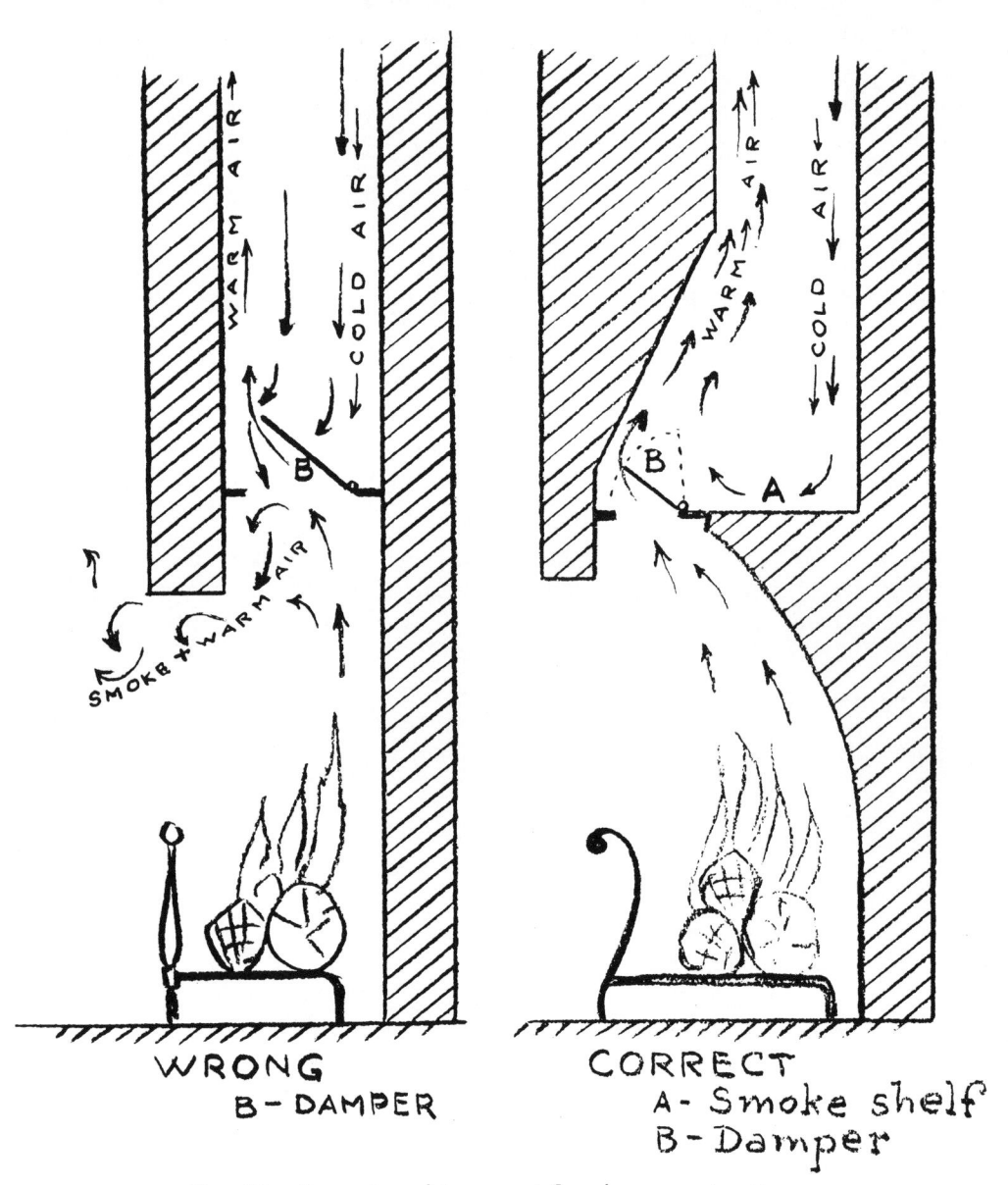

Fig. 10. Correct and incorrect fireplace construction.

pleasant an appearance, you might do well to face the exposed surface of the foundation walls with stone, which will blend well with the logs.

Under ordinary conditions it is not necessary to provide for anchoring the sill logs to the piers or foundation walls. However, if you are building in an area where tornadoes and violent storms are known to occur it might be advisable to set bolts into the top of your foundation. The decision is up to the individual builder.

For a basement, the walls are built like any other walls with enough surface at the top to allow for a cement or plaster edge along the sill log (Fig. 9). This is designed to shed water. It is a good idea to creosote the sill logs if they rest on piers below the floor level. Creosote has a rather strong odor which is quite offensive to some people. Therefore, although it is an excellent preservative, it should be used below or directly over the ground.

The Fireplace

A log cabin would not be a log cabin without a fireplace. There are any number of effective designs for fireplaces. If you study a few you can plan one of your own. Although I recommend that you have a mason do the actual work, it is important that you understand the basic principles of fireplace construction.

The base of the fireplace must be sturdy because it will have to support a great weight of stone. It must reach below the frost line, just as the piers. If there is a basement, the base of the fireplace will be part of the foundation and the hearth can be built up between the floor joists as in any other home. In case there is no basement, of course, a hole will have to be dug. The base is built up to within about 4 in. of the floor level. Large stones are used for filler and rods for reinforcement. A wood form, of course, will have to be used for the section above the ground.

Figure 10 shows the correct design of a fireplace to obtain proper

Fig. 11. Sheet-iron fireplace unit.

Fig. 12. Opening for fireplace.

Fig. 13. Fireplace built into opening such as shown in Fig. 12. The chimney will be outside.

draft. This basic construction is requisite for a fireplace to draw well and throw out heat. The smoke is carried by the warm air through the throat and up the flue. Note that the cold air seeks its way down the flue but that the smoke shelf prevents it from forcing smoke into the room by deflecting it upward. The damper helps to throw the cold downdraft of the flue upward. When the fireplace is not in use the damper is closed to prevent unwelcome visitors from entering the cabin.

A sheet-iron fireplace unit is shown in Figure 11. Various makes are on the market. This one is called a Heatolator and usually can be obtained from larger hardware dealers and firms specializing in fireplace equipment. Stone and brick can be masoned around it. Hot-air registers at the top and the bottom throw added heat into the room.

There are different methods of building up the chimney. One is to allow a gap in the logs as the walls are erected and then to build the fireplace and chimney into that space (Fig. 12). The fireplace is then built into the opening as in Figure 13. In this case the chimney will be on the outside. Another method is simpler to my way of thinking. It consists of building up the entire fireplace and chimney before the walls or any

Fig. 14. Fireplace with sides grooved for logs.

logs are laid. Obviously the workmen have much more freedom. A groove is left down the sides of the chimney into which the ends of the logs are fitted (Fig. 14). It is much easier to get the ends of the logs into this recess than to fit the chimney to the logs. If the chimney is built last, the projecting logs must be cut to shape at the opening and must be held in place by a couple of heavy planks (Fig. 12). Some builders construct the walls and fireplace simultaneously.

The fireplace can be faced on all sides with cut stone, flagstone, round boulders, or brick. Your selection will depend on the material available and your individual preferences. Common brick, new or old, makes a fine fireplace for a log cabin. Split field stone seems to be everyone's choice, but it must be laid up correctly to look right. The use of stones of several contrasting colors does not produce a very beautiful effect. It is much better to use different shades of one color, whether they run to grays or browns or whatever is to be had in your locality. A gaudy fireplace is just as out of place in a log cabin as chromium or crystal lighting fixtures.

The fireplace proper, that is the place where the fire will be, is to be lined with firebrick set in fire clay. Stones should not be used because with the extreme changes in temperature they flake off and often explode. In some localities native stone is especially lacking in heat-resisting qualities.

The hearth, the floor of the fireplace, is laid after the floor of the cabin. It is usually set in concrete. A layer of rather "dry" mixed cement is laid over the entire area and flagstones or other flat stones are set level with the floor. A 3 to 1 mortar is poured and troweled between them. Brick also can be used and will provide a fine level surface.

Chimney erected and sill logs in place.

In Figure 13 the chimney is on the outside of the cabin. The chimney of the fireplace on this page is visible both on the inside and the outside. Some chimneys of this type are built wide enough to occupy the better portion of the wall area.

One method of building the roof around the chimney.

Chapter 5

WALLS

By this time your tract will have been cleared and the foundation (piers, foundation wall, or basement) built. The fireplace, if you have followed the author's recommendation, now stands high above the site and you are ready to begin the most intriguing part of the job, laying up the logs.

Sill and End Logs

First of all the logs should be spread out on the ground so that you can see them all. Much time and effort is saved if you are able to select them as you need them without turning over the entire pile. Pick out the two largest and straightest for the sill logs, that is, the first logs for the long sides, and lay them on the piers or foundation wall. The butts should be at opposite ends. In other words, if the butt end of one faces north, the other should face south. Note well that as the walls are built, the butt ends are to be alternated in this manner so that the walls will be level. The logs, of course, are cut out flat where they rest on the piers to provide a firm frame on which to build. For foundation walls the sill logs are hewed flat the full length of the surface on which they are to rest. With the two sill logs placed solidly on the foundation, the end logs are now notched to them and laid in place. There is a space equal to the thickness of a half log between these logs and the tops of the piers (Fig. 15). To prevent sagging, the tops of the piers under these logs are built up to the logs with concrete.

The floor joists can be laid either before or after the walls (see Chap. 8, Floors, Stairs, and Ceilings). It is advisable to build the floor last because while working on the inside, joists are very much in the way. Walking over them is troublesome and laying loose boards over them is dangerous. You will be better off, therefore, leaving the ground to walk on until the walls are built, and the debris, incidently, will be easily removed. Of course, if there is a basement below the house, joists and a subfloor must be laid before the walls are put up, as in any other building.

Joints

Many different methods of joining logs are used in log-cabin construction. Some are employed for their appearance. Others are preferred for strength and economy. Only a few basic ones will be described here.

Fig. 15. Sill and end log in place.

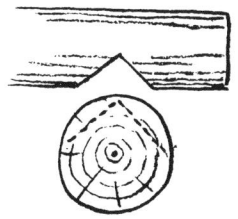

Fig. 16. A-and-V joint.

Fig. 17. Common joint.

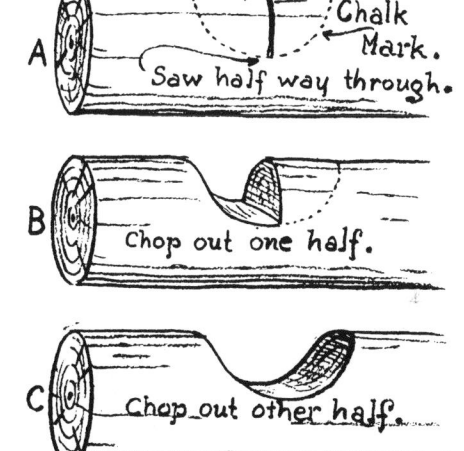

Fig. 18. Method of notching for common joint.

A-and-V Joint

The A-and-V joint shown in Figure 16 is recommended for small logs. A minimum of wood is removed with the result that the projecting ends are not unduly weakened. The entire joint is made with a hand ax. The lower log is spiked after it has been cut out.

Common Joint

The common method of notching logs for an accurate fit is shown in

[31]

Laying up walls using the A-and-V joint.

Preparing a common joint with an adz.

Figure 17. It is rather simple. Examine the log so that the best side or face will be on the inside of the cabin. Then mark both sides and both ends with a marking gauge. As shown in Figure 6, the gauge is set to about the middle of the log to be cut, if you want the logs to touch, and the arc is marked. If the log is inclined to roll, have someone hold it in place. Now turn the log upside down and cut along this line with a large gouge and mallet to a depth of about an inch and pry away the wood. Then with an ax or adz cut out the remaining wood. A saw cut down the center as shown in Figure 18 will make this operation much simpler. Too much time would be required to complete the notch with a gouge. If you have marked correctly and cut to the line, the log will plop in place like the cover on a trunk. Each corner is secured with a couple of 60-penny nails.

Perhaps you prefer ax-cut ends to saw-cut ends (Fig. 19). The former add a beautiful rustic touch. If you are a good ax man and like such ends it is your privilege to make them. Personally I'll take the saw-cut type because there is less danger of rotting due to absorption of water.

You will observe in some of the drawings that there is space between the logs. Some builders, however, prefer to have the logs touch each other. Whether one method is more advisable than another is a matter of opinion.

If space is left between the logs the corners true up better, the walls can be erected faster, and one or two logs can be saved on each wall. These spaces can be filled easily by chinking.

Be sure that the logs on the inside of the wall are in the best possible alignment. Figure 20, while somewhat exaggerated, shows how they should be lined up.

Dovetail Joint

The dovetail joint (Fig. 22) is sometimes used, especially if projecting ends must be eliminated. Sometimes it is used for all corners to save logs. About 2 ft. can be gained on each log with dovetail ends. The procedure for making this joint is shown in Figure 21. First the cutting line is marked off with chalk or crayon. Then a notch is sawed or chopped and the remaining wood is split off with a froe or ax. If the tongue is equal to the thickness of half the log as shown in Figure 21, the logs should touch along their full length provided they are straight. If the tongue is more than half the thickness of the log, there will be a space between the logs. All irregular spots and all knots must be smoothed off with an ax or an adz if the logs are to fit tightly.

Fig. 19. Ax-cut ends.

Fig. 20. Logs aligned on inside of cabin.

[33]

Fig. 21. Method of cutting dovetail joint.

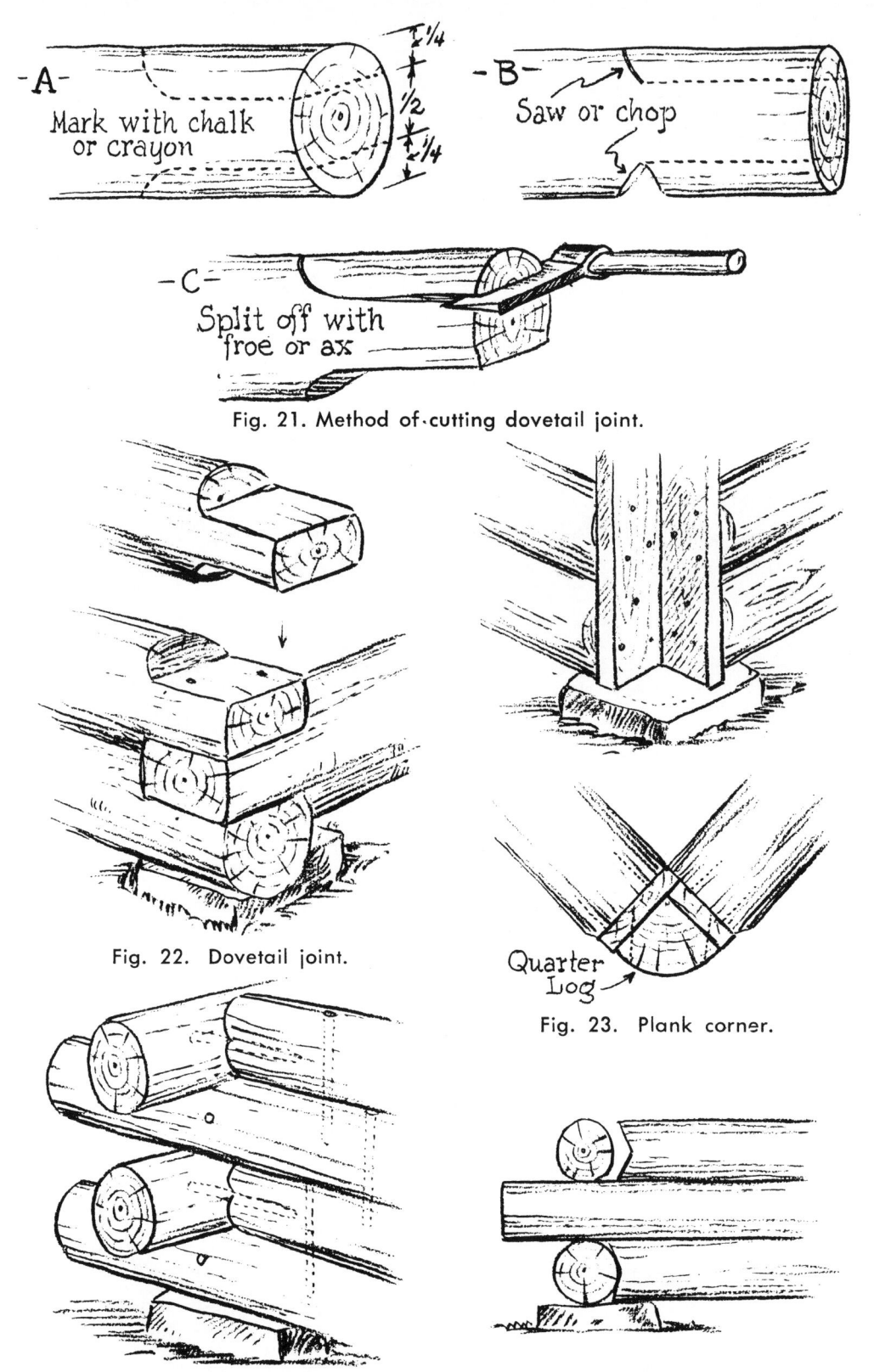

Fig. 22. Dovetail joint.

Fig. 23. Plank corner.

Fig. 24. Butt joint with logs secured by rods or dowels.

[34]

Other Methods

Where logs are rather scarce, the method shown in Figure 24 can be employed. This joint eliminates much chopping but it is not as artistic as those explained above. The logs are held together with long iron rods or hardwood dowels. Inasmuch as no notching is done, the logs must be pinned together with care.

Figure 23 shows another method which makes a very neat corner. For small cabins each of the four walls can be assembled on the ground and then set up after which the corners are spiked. Care must be taken so that every wall will be absolutely square. This method saves log footage and is faster than any other, for which reason it is practical for auto-camp cottages and the like.

Door and Window Openings

If logs are plentiful, the logs can be built up to the top sill and then the openings for the doors and windows can be cut out. First guide strips are nailed in place as shown in Figure 25. These will also serve as braces to hold the logs in position after they are sawed. Then the frames of 2 by 6- or 2 by 8-in. planks are fitted and nailed into and against the ends of the logs and set in at the bottom as shown in Figure 26. The size of the openings and the frames for the windows will, of course, depend on the dimensions of the sashes, which should be purchased before you start to build.

Fig. 25. Sawing out window and door openings.

Fig. 26. Frame nailed to ends of logs.

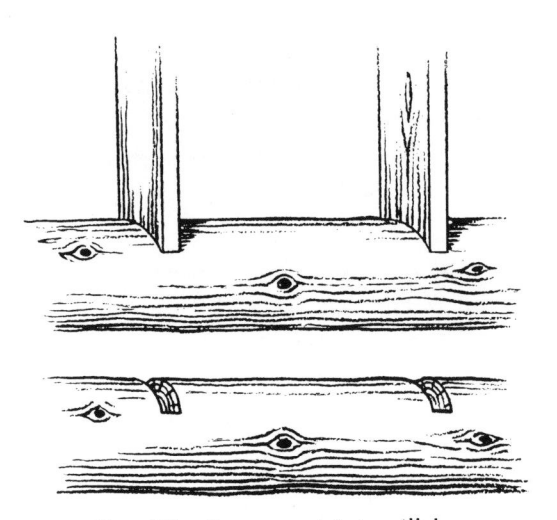

Fig. 27. Frame set into sill log.

Fig. 28. Door frame braced and ready to be set.

Fig. 29. Door frame set and properly braced.

Fireplaces

The logs can be cut to allow necessary openings as the walls are being erected. The opening for a fireplace of the type shown in Figure 13 is illustrated in Figure 12. If the full length of the chimney is to show on the inside of the cabin, the logs are cut from the bottom to the top of the wall. If the fireplace and the chimney are put up first, the logs are cut to fit around it.

Doors

Provision for the openings for the doors is shown in Figures 27, 28, and 29. Slots are cut in the sill log and the lower ends of the door frame are set into them and toenailed. The frames are braced crosswise to keep them square. This type of bracing is shown in Figure 28. Do not remove these braces until all the logs are laid. Two stout supports also should be nailed to the side of the frame as shown in Figure 29 to hold it upright. Be sure that the frame is absolutely plumb. Thus it will act as a true perpendicular guide when laying up the logs because they are aligned with the inner edge of the planks.

Here I would like to insert an important note of caution. Be sure that the log ends which fit against window and door frames are cut square. If only *one* log is cut too short the long 40- or 60-penny spikes will pull the frame out of line. On the other hand, a log that is *too long* will cause a bulge in the frame. A miter-box arrangement as shown in Figure 30 is effective for cutting log ends square. If a log is too short, do not attempt to pull it in place. The frame will be moved out of plumb and a bulge will be produced. The next log may spring out just a bit more and then you will have trouble on your hands. Remember, once frames are in, they are in for good. Frames have the strength to hold a wall rigidly true. For best appearance, the planks should be the same width as the logs or slightly narrower, as shown in Figure 26.

Windows

The walls are now laid up to the level of the window sills. Do not forget to alternate the butt ends.

Now make the window frames as shown in Figure 31. For this purpose 2 by 6- or 2 by 8-in. planks can be used. They are squared up and braced as the door frames were.

To determine the height at which to set the window frames refer to Figure 32, which shows a door frame and a window frame. As a rule the tops of the windows and doors are at the same level. Thus there will be

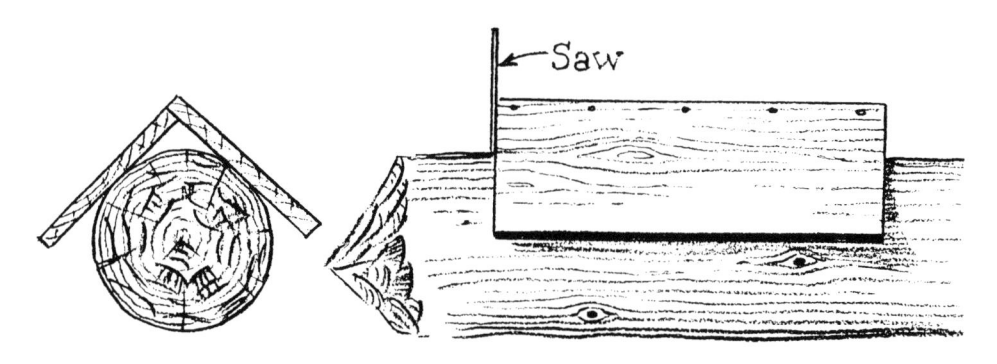

Fig. 30. Guide for cutting log ends square.

Fig. 31. Braced window frame.

no break in the log immediately above the door and window openings, which makes for rigid construction. So be governed by the height of the doors. The sill of the window frame sets on or is recessed into the logs depending on dimensions. In the same drawing the log has been cut out to accommodate the window frame.

Fig. 32. Tops of window and door frames aligned.

[38]

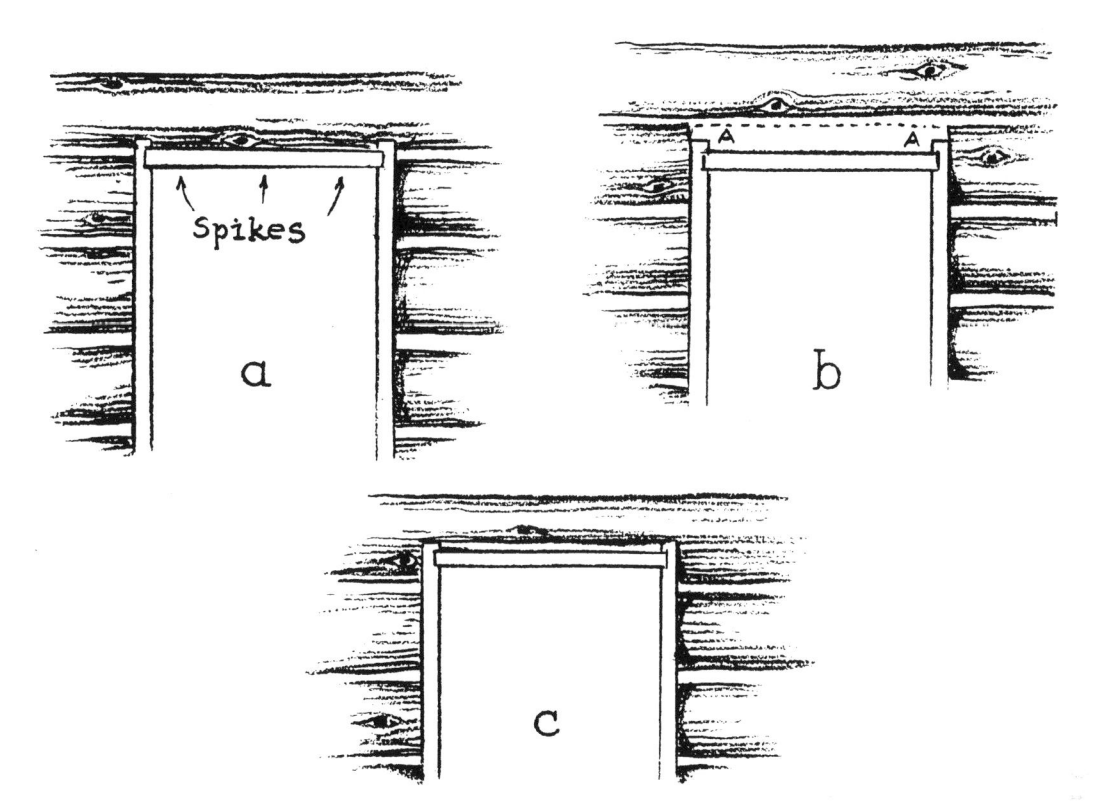

Fig. 33. How window frames may fit.

Fig. 34. Window trim.

[39]

Laying up walls.

The frame in Figure 33A fits very accurately. The top meets the log above it as it should. The top plank can be spiked to the upper log. However, an imperfect fit is more likely to occur. In Figure 33B the frame does not reach the upper log. The space A–A in such a case can be filled with a section of log or plaster. In Figure 33C the top log has been cut out for the frame. There should be at least one continuous log above the frames depending on the height of the wall.

If you have the time and energy you can do a little extra trimming around the window and door frames with half logs mitered at the corners. Ceder fence posts often are used for this purpose (see Fig. 34). The wall logs may have to be trimmed to fit the half logs. The places where the ends of the wall logs touch should be filled with plaster or cement. Your only problem involved in using half logs is ripping them. They are too small to be ripped in a sawmill and usually are too large for a table saw. Outside of cutting them by hand with a course rip saw, the only machine that can be used is a band saw. And if the band saw has a narrow blade, the half logs will require planing to true up the cut.

Ceilings and Second Floors

The walls of small cabins, as a rule, are not built much higher than one log above the tops of the window and door frames. However, one or more logs can be added if higher walls are desired. If there is to be no ceiling proper, that is, if the roof is to constitute the ceiling, you can now proceed to lay the roof rafters.

If a ceiling is to be built as shown in Figure 36, the joists are now notched as in Figure 35 and spiked to the plate logs. Ceiling joists should be spaced about 18 in. apart to centers if a second story is to be added, or from 3 to 4 ft. apart if they will not have to bear much weight. They are leveled and the ceiling of matched lumber is laid on top of them. The roof is then put on. However, if the wall is one or two logs higher than the level of the ceiling, you will have ample room to lay the floor after the roof is up. The important reason for building the roof before laying the floor, whenever possible, is that even a light shower may permanently warp the floor.

If your cabin is to be a story and a half (Fig. 37) or two stories high, the joists are set, the walls are built up to the desired height, and the roof is put on. The floor, or ceiling, can then be laid. The joists either can be set into the wall logs as shown in Figure 37 or the ends can project a foot or so as indicated by the dotted lines.

When building a cabin without a ceiling that is more than 15 ft., it may be advisable to lay one or more joists between the walls to prevent them from spreading in the midsection under the weight of the roof or snow.

Chinking

Chinking is the process of filling up the open space between logs. It is necessary to exclude vermin and insects and to keep the cabin dry and comfortable. This is one of the most important operations in building a log cabin. The logs should be dry when chinking is done. Otherwise you will have a job of caulking or rechinking to do in a year or so due to the shrinkage of the logs. Logs and lumber, however, shrink only in diameter.

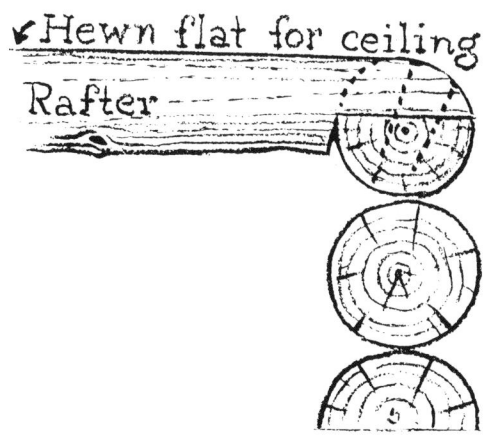

Fig. 35. Ceiling rafter notched into plate log.

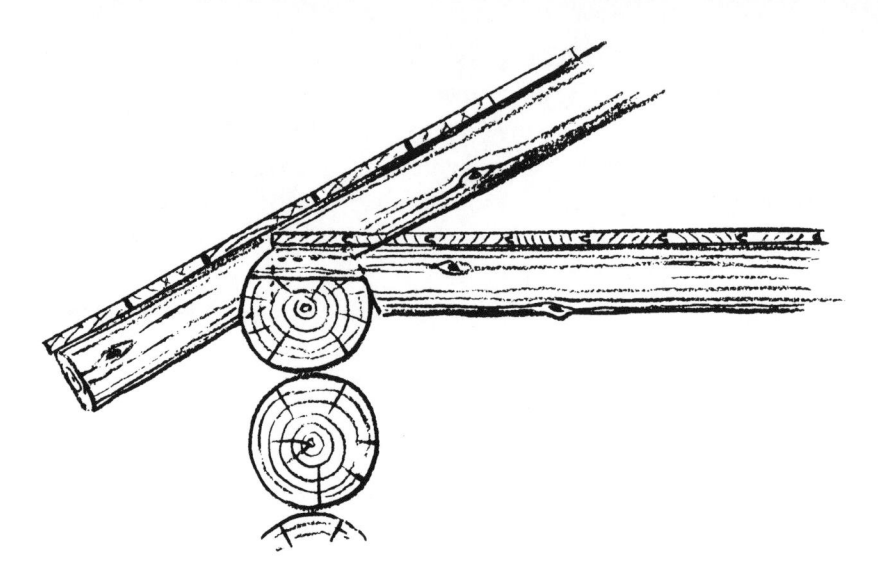

Fig. 36. Construction of ceiling where no storage space is required.

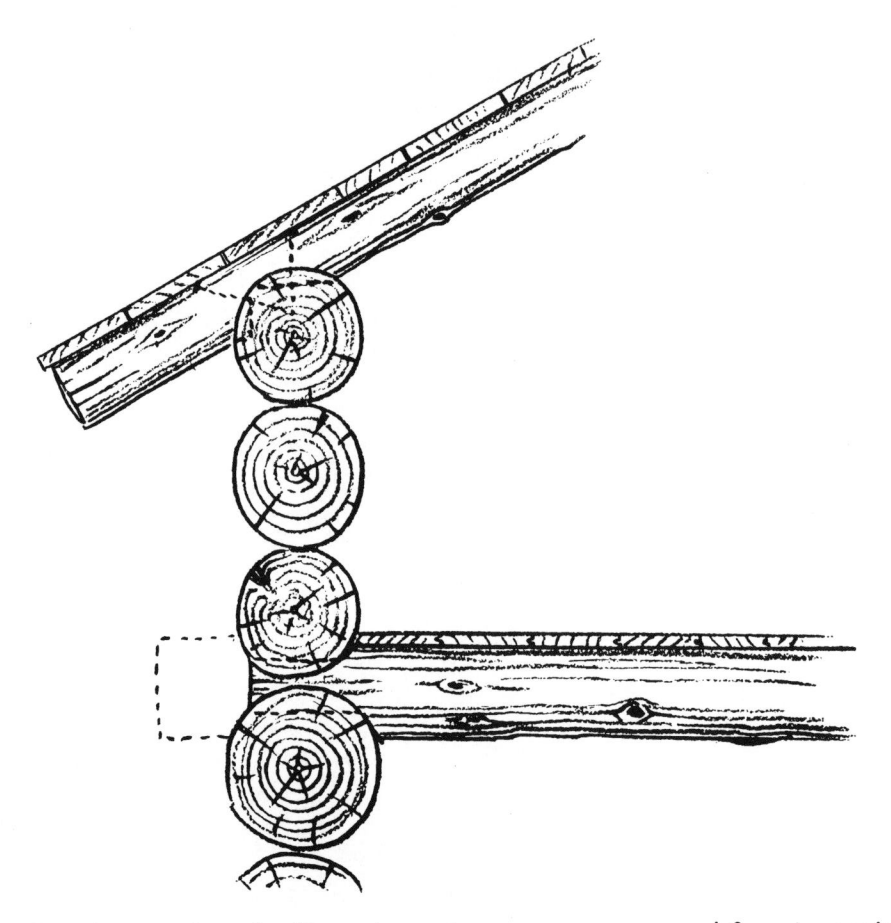

Fig. 37. Construction of ceiling where storage space or second floor is required.

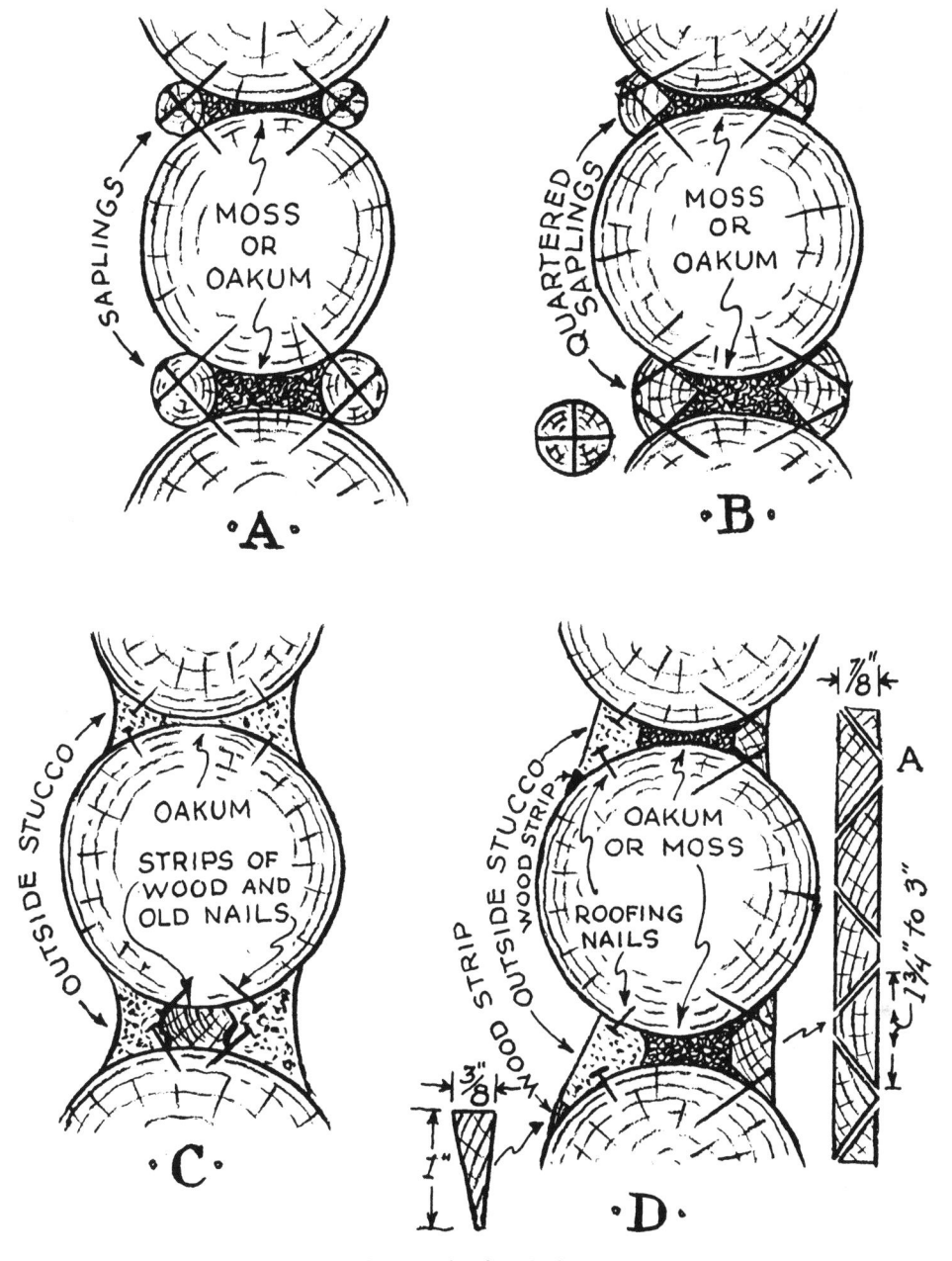

Fig. 38. Methods of chinking.

Chinking Material

In the Ozark Mountains mud or clay is commonly used for chinking. "Mud dauber" is the name applied to one who does this sort of work. Strips of wood are tacked in larger openings and the clay is worked to proper consistency and applied by hand. Thinner clay is later used to fill the cracks. Rain, of course, will wash out mud.

[43]

Sphagnum moss is sometimes used in the far north or wherever it is found. If not protected by chinking strips, however, it will dry up and will be pulled out by chipmunks, rats, and even birds.

Oakum is an excellent chinking material because it repells rats and bugs. It, too, requires reinforcement.

Plaster cement or mortar withstands weather better than anything else. A good mixture can be made of 3 parts Portland cement, 3 parts of clean washed sand, and 1 part of hydrated lime. It should be mixed so that it can be worked into cracks and small openings, and fill large openings without sagging. Several excellent prepared mortars are on the market. They are supplied in 100-lb. paper bags and only require mixing with water. Use an outside stucco plaster for the exterior and a wood mortar for the interior of the cabin. It is advisable to have a supply on hand, but it should be stored in a dry place. Incidentally, ready-mixed mortar is available for laying brick and stone also. It saves a lot of work.

Chinking is required whether the logs are set tight or whether there is space between them. In the case of the former, there may be a spline between the logs or the bottoms of the logs may be hollowed out to fit over the logs below. Both types of fitting require caulking. Oakum and in some places sphagnum moss, protected by some sort of wood or plaster shield, is used. Walls that are not solid require other methods. These are shown in Figure 38.

The simplest method of chinking is shown in Figure 38A. A thin sapling is nailed between the logs on the outside. Then sphagnum moss is driven between the logs from the inside and another sapling is nailed on the inside. These saplings may be peeled or not depending on the preference of the builder. Green saplings will form themselves to the surfaces to which they are nailed much better than dry ones. After drying out, however, they must be driven down tight again.

Figure 38B shows the same method with the exception that the saplings are cut into quarters. This makes a much neater job. This method and the above are common in the north where plaster is scarce. They are also employed if a fast job is in order.

Plaster is used for the chinking job shown in Figure 38C. Outside stucco plaster is very good for this purpose. Some builders drive a piece of metal lath between the logs and secure it with nails to anchor the plaster. For this purpose nails can also be driven into the logs as shown in the illustration. This method has been used with great success by the author.

Where there are large openings pieces of wood can be driven between the logs. These are nailed in place and plaster is spread over them. The plaster should be applied with a trowel and smoothed out in the form of a fillet with the hands. A pair of leather gloves will be found helpful.

Figure 38D shows a method employed in some sections of the Rocky Mountains. Instead of saplings, wedge-shaped strips cut out of 1-in. board as shown are driven between the logs and nailed in place on the inside of the cabin. If the wedges are wet they will fit over irregularities much better. Moss or oakum is forced between the logs from the outside. Next, a small, wedge-shaped strip of wood is nailed to each log on the outside as a retaining shelf for the fillet of plaster which is then applied.

The method last described is the neatest and most practical according to the writer's experience. The inside strips eliminate plaster, which frequently flakes off and causes needless dirt. The appearance of the interior will be greatly enhanced if the chinking strips are of the same wood as the logs. When the walls are oiled or waxed the wood will have a uniform color. The wedge-shaped strips on the outside make a substantial job because they prevent the plaster from feathering out and breaking off.

Finishing the Logs

The inner walls should be as clean and bright as possible. Dark logs will produce a dark interior. Moreover, the logs should make an even-colored wall. With enough help the logs can be drawknifed on the inner surface as they are laid. First notch the log and fit it. Then roll it a quarter turn, that is, have the inner side uppermost; get someone to hold it steady, or wedge it; and shave off the inner surface. Then lay the log in position and spike it down. Thus the inside surface of your logs will be clean when laid up. To keep them in good condition put the roof on as soon as possible. Sun and rain will darken freshly shaved wood. Oil will not prevent discoloration if the logs are exposed too long to the weather.

To make a real job of it, the face of each chinking strip should be hand-planed with a slightly curved blade so that plane marks will show. There is no hurry about this, however, because the roof will be on when you are doing this work.

Drawknifing log before notching.

Some persons like to have the outside look like the inside. The logs, of course, will have to be drawknifed and later oiled and varnished. Individual preferences vary widely in this matter. I prefer an exterior with a natural weather color. I have seen some cabins painted brown with cream log ends, but I often wondered why the owner ever wanted a lob cabin in the first place. Again I have seen entire interiors lathed and plastered. But these are extreme cases. A log cabin ceases to be a log cabin with such modifications. But the rustic beauty of the true log cabin appeals so much to the average person that no defense of it need be made here.

Chapter 6

ROOFS

In planning the roof, the builder must consider its pitch and the projection of the eaves and the ridge. Practical advantages as well as artistic effect should be carefully weighed.

The roofs of log cabins as a rule do not have very much pitch. The average pitch or slope is about 5 in. to the foot. If it is much less than this, rain may drive in under the shingles.

Two common types of roof construction are shown in Figures 39 and 40. In Figure 39 the roof is supported by members running the length of the cabin. They are laid as the gable ends are built up and spiked at the ends. The small openings at the roof line are chinked later with plaster or wood or both.

The logs used for this purpose should be at least 8 in. in diameter especially in places that have heavy snowfalls. If the cabin is more than 12 or 14 ft. in length it may be necessary to build braces, like those in Figure 41, midway between the two end walls. If the room is very long such supports should be constructed about 8 to 10 ft. apart.

The roof boards run up and down with an overhang of 12 to 24 in. Before they are laid, a long, straight-edged board should be placed across the roof rafters to detect high spots. All of these should be leveled with a drawknife so that the roof boards can be set evenly in place. If wood shingles are to be used, the boards should be placed ¼ in. apart. This spacing will permit the shingles to dry both from the top and bottom. If composition material or tar paper is to be used for the roof, the boards should be laid closely together, or better still, matched lumber is recommended.

Figure 40 shows the gable end of a roof supported by rafters. The logs used for the rafters should be about 6 in. at the butt. The rafters are set no more than 2 ft. apart. They are notched to the plate log as shown in Figure 42 and spiked. At the top the rafters are spiked to the ridge board. A 1-in. board will serve as a ridge board. The roof boards in this case run lengthwise. They, too, should be spaced ¼ to ½ in. apart if wood shingles are used, or closer together for composition or tar paper roofs.

Figure 40 also shows a method of closing up the gable ends. Wide boards or slabs can be used for this purpose. For weatherproofing they can be covered on the inside with a sheet of insulating board or heavy

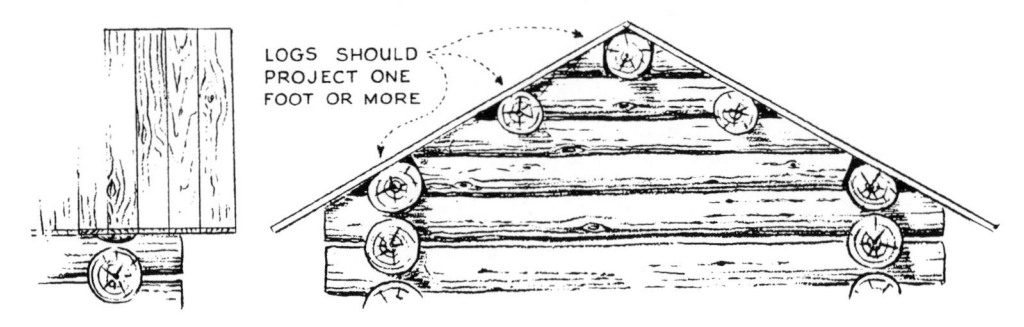

Fig. 39. Roof supported by horizontal members.

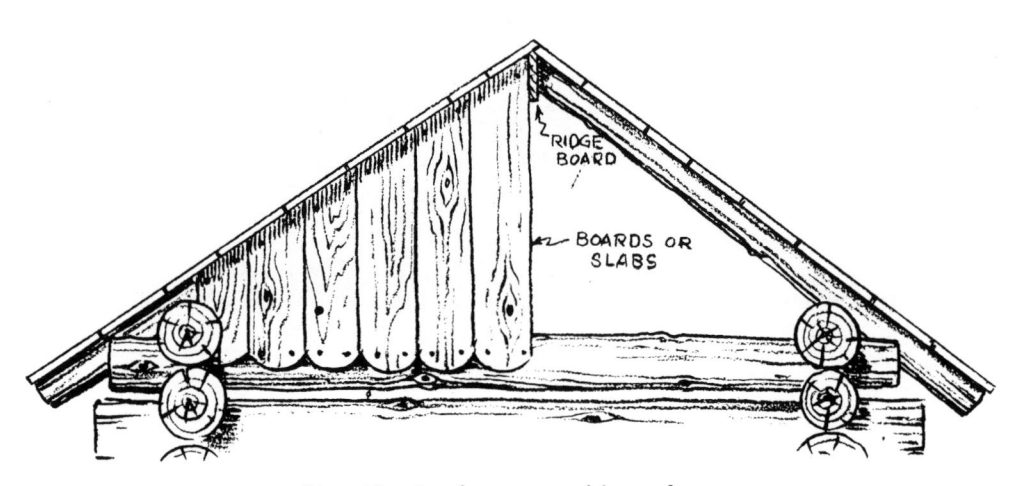

Fig. 40. Roof supported by rafters.

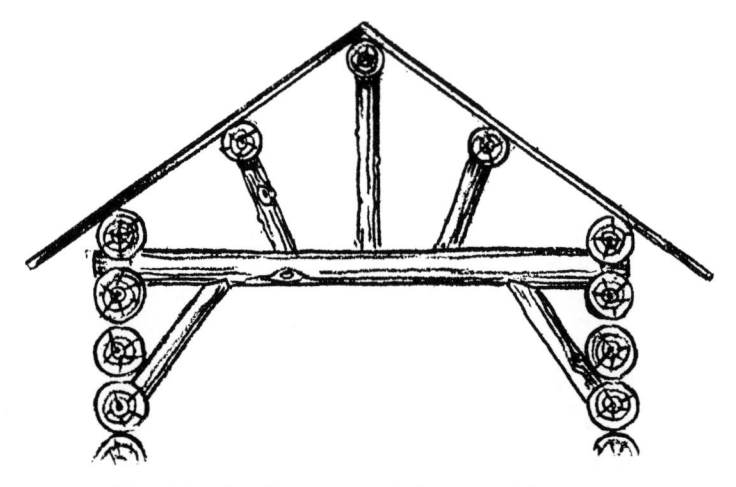

Fig. 41. Roof supported by special braces.

[48]

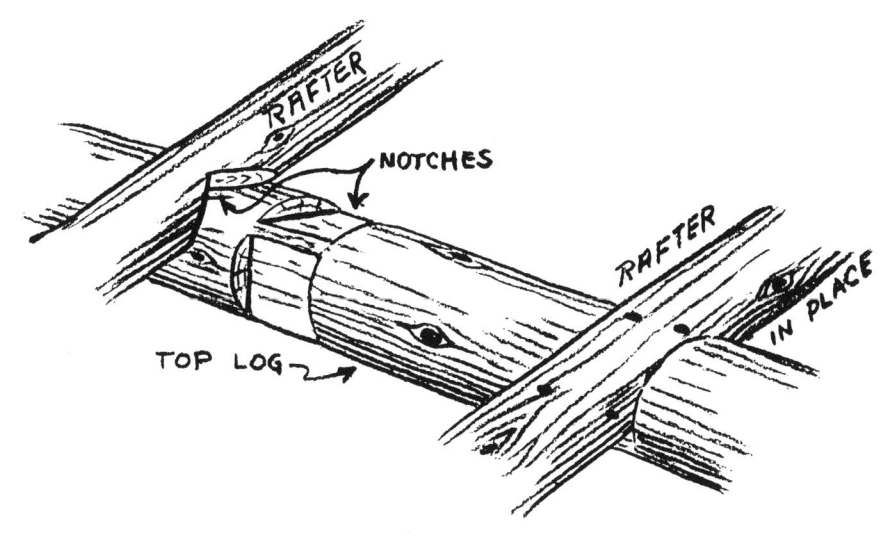

Fig. 42. Rafters notched into plate log.

building paper or they may be backed with other boards running up and down. Battens can be nailed over the cracks if the cabin is only used for camping purposes.

Flashing

Flashing is metal such as tin, copper, or galvanized sheet iron used to waterproof the roof where it meets the chimney, roof valleys (places where two roofs meet), etc. Chimney flashing is bent at right angles, tacked to the roof boards, and the upper edge of the portion which rests against the chimney is set into the mortar. The drawing below shows how flashing is set

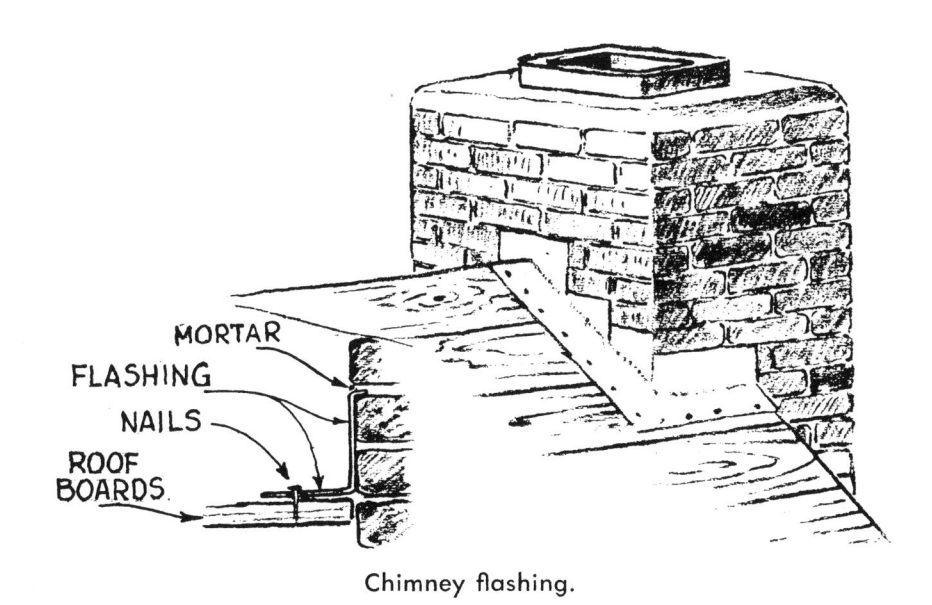

Chimney flashing.

[49]

Rafters laid.

into a brick chimney. The roofing material is laid over the flashing and the edges are sealed with roofing compound. If the flashing consists of more than one piece of metal, be sure to allow sufficient overlap, or solder the joints. The laps can be sealed with roofing cement if no soldering equipment is available. Flashing usually is set into the mortar when the chimney is going up through the roof. If the chimney is built first, the mortar is chipped out where the flashing is to be set in. The edge of the flashing is then bent and set into the chimney and sealed with plaster. Chimney flashing should extend at least 4 in. beneath the shingles. Flashing for valleys should be at least 8 in. wide, which allows 4 in. for each side of the valley.

Roofing Material

Most cabins have low-pitched roofs. This feature makes them picturesque but at the same time the job of rainproofing them is more difficult. Wood shingles on this type of roof have a tendency to leak. Hence, a good grade of composition roll or strip shingle roofing is recommended. This material is not only waterproof but is also very easy to apply. If the roof has a somewhat steep pitch, ordinary hand-split cedar or cypress shingles can be used. Figure 43 shows how shingles are split with a froe.

Roof Patching

It is a good policy to have a can of roofing cement on hand. This is a thick asphalt preparation which can be applied with a putty knife or common table knife. It is excellent for repairing holes in roofing, sealing chimney flashing, caulking around windows, and so on. Once you use it you will wonder how the old timers got along without it. Roofing cement also can be used to plug up mouse holes and to repair damage done by squirrels. They will not relish the taste of this material. And in inclement weather if you observe a bad spot in the chinking or chimney flashing you can make a good temporary repair by plugging it up with oakum and applying a coat of this cement.

Fig. 43. Splitting shingles with a froe.

Chapter 7

WINDOWS, DOORS, AND SHUTTERS

Windows

There are three types of windows commonly used in log cabins which a layman can easily fit. They are regular double-hung windows, casement windows, and tilting windows. The double-hung window is illustrated in Figure 44. Note the 2-in. plank casing or frame. The upper and lower sash should fit together as indicated. The stops, however, need not be rabbeted into the frame but can be nailed. These windows have no weights; they are held open and locked shut with window springbolts like the one in Figure 47. Figure 34 shows how these windows appear from the outside. This type of window was used in the old log cabin built of square-hewn oak logs that was mentioned before and in the first section of the author's cabin.

Casement windows are more simple to install, but in my estimation they are not as weatherproof, unless one wishes to go to the expense and trouble of installing bronze weather stripping. Figure 45 is a sectional view of a casement window. Figure 48 shows how weather stripping can be applied at the bottom to keep out wind-driven rain at the sill. It should be noted that if these weather strips are too tight they will bind when wet, and if too loose they will leak. Casement windows swing inward and can be locked by means of ordinary casement-window latches. A good feature of casement windows is that they can be washed on both sides from the inside of the cabin.

The tilting window in Figure 46 is also rather simple to install. The upper section opens inward like a transom for ventilation while the lower sash is tight. Windows of this type are used in one of the sections of my cabin and are 40 in. wide.

I would like to say again at this time that log cabins as a rule are rather dark unless adequate fenestration is provided. If there is an exceptionally beautiful view from one or two sides of your cabin, it would be well to set in a large 6- or 8-ft. plate glass "picture window." Since these windows are large and heavy they will be stationary, so that ventilation will have to be supplied by means of doors and other windows. Picture windows, it is true, are not very rustic; in fact they are what might be termed ultramodern. However, they can do much to brighten up a cabin. And with

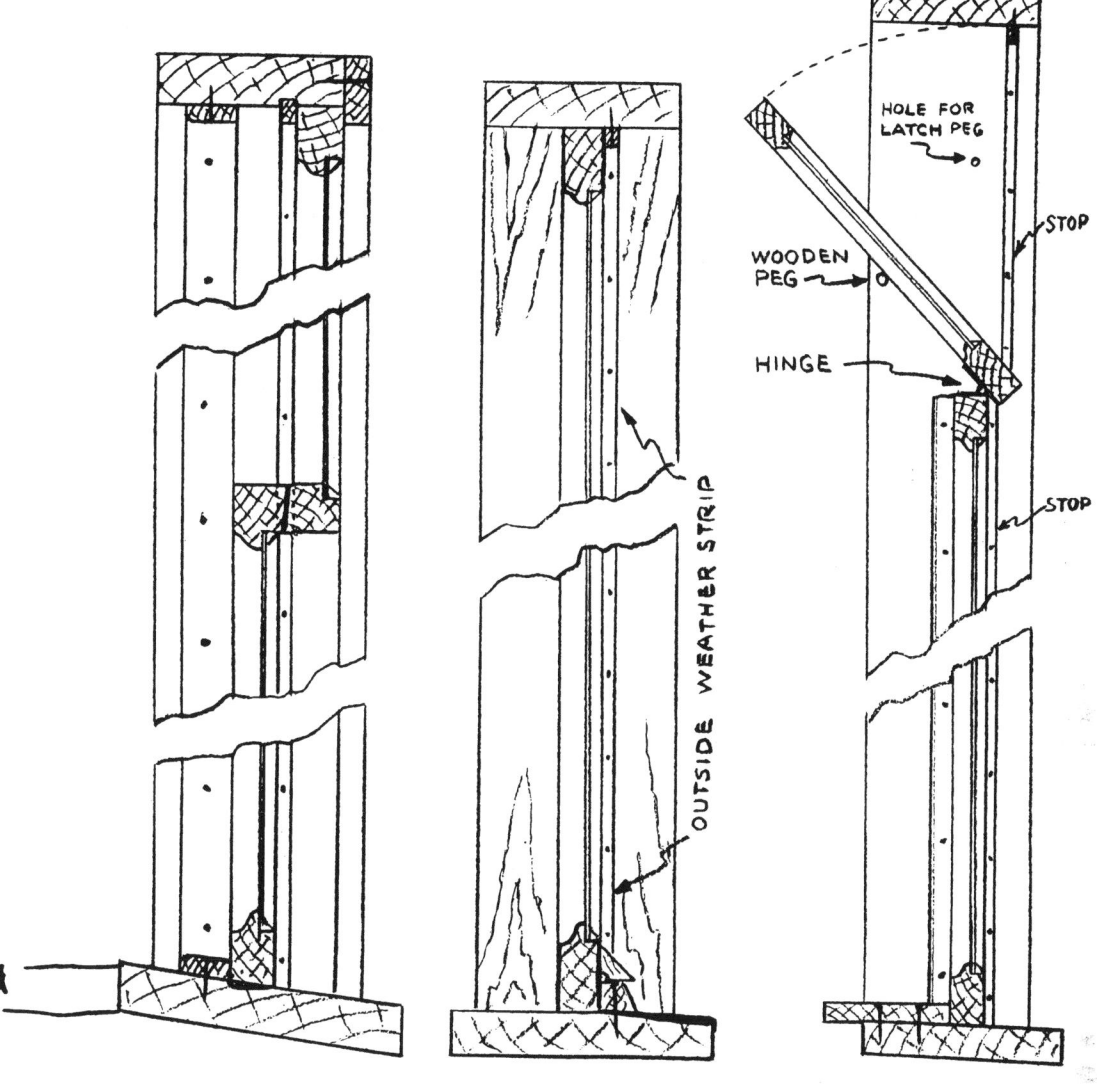

Fig. 44. Double-hung window.

Fig. 45. Casement window.

Fig. 46. Tilting window.

Fig. 47. Spring bolt for double-hinge window.

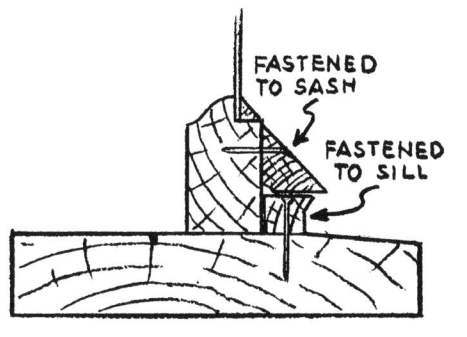

Fig. 48. Weather stripping for casement window.

[53]

Fig. 49. Door made with matched lumber.

Fig. 50. Door made with splines.

a picture window overlooking a mountain range, a lake, or river, or even a woodland view you can bring the great outdoors, indoors. Be sure to have enough roof overhang to keep the window as clear as possible at all times.

Doors

It has been pointed out already that one will find doors made of matched fencing lumber in some of the old log cabins that date back sixty or more years. Doors of this construction are still in existence. While they were not particularly strong, they served their purpose. Today they are used frequently as inside doors. Wainscot lumber also makes good inside doors.

Perhaps the best doors for log cabins are those made of 1¼- or 1½-in. dressed pine planks. Figure 49 shows a door made of such lumber with tongue-and-groove construction. Battens hold the planks together. Tongues and grooves are cut with a dado or with a special plane. Ready-made doors of this type can be ordered from a millwork company. Splines also

[54]

can be used as in Figure 50. The doors shown in the photograph on page 63 were of this construction. The planks may be from 6 to 10 in. wide. These drawings show the inside of the doors. For battens 2 by 4-in. board is used, which usually measures 1½ by 3½ in. when dressed. They are fastened to the boards with 2½-in. lag screws, large wood screws, or large, square, iron cut nails. Lead holes should be drilled first irrespective of the method used and the planks should be clamped together while being fastened. The edges of each plank can be given a ¼ in. chamfer.

Very fine doors can be made of 1¼ by 3½-in. fir porch flooring. This material is tongued and grooved. If only ¾-in. lumber is on hand, a good outside door can be made similar to the batten door, described above, except that the top and bottom battens are flush with the top and bottom edges of the door. Three-inch batten strips are nailed along the two sides flush with the edges and two 2-in. battens are crossed from corner to corner. Then the side reinforced with battens is covered with ¾-in. lumber making a solid looking door 1¼ in. thick.

Slabs make even a more picturesque door. The method of construction is the same. They are peeled and drawknifed evenly so that they all have the same general appearance. The battens are fastened on the flat side.

Dutch doors.

If no tongues and grooves are cut, the cracks are sealed by means of ¼ by 1¼-in. batten strips.

Perhaps you prefer Dutch doors like those which are shown on page 55. The upper section may or may not have a window as desired. This is a very functional door. The top half can be opened for ventilation and the lower half can be left latched. Latches should be installed on both lower and upper sections of an outside Dutch door. There should also be a bolt latch to fasten the upper to the lower half. Cross battens should slant from the lower hinge edge to the upper latch edge as shown in the drawings. They keep the door from sagging.

Shutters

The northern trapper used to leave his latch string out so that anyone in need of shelter would have access to his cabin. His place was locked, or rather latched, only against marauding animals. But in the highly civilized world today it is unwise to let a cabin stand in the woods without some sort of protection. As a rule some neighbors will keep an eye on it when it is not occupied. Nevertheless, ordinary precautions should be taken to safeguard your home. The doors should have good Yale locks in addition to latches. The windows require adequate protection. Even window screens are of some help, not much to be sure, but a little. A cabin that is not used during the fall and winter should be shuttered. The shutters can be made of 1-in. boards. They can either be hinged or secured with common wing fasteners like screens and storm windows. In either case they should be flush with the window frame, that is, set into the frames and fastened with hooks on the inside. It is not as easy to pry off a flush shutter as it is to pull off one that projects beyond the window frame. There are those who will say that if one wishes to break into a place there is nothing that will stop them. True, but remember, a boarded up home is not as inviting as a cozy little den with shades up and interior neatly appointed. And if a home is a little difficult to enter the thief or vandal will hesitate before trying.

Chapter 8

FLOORS, STAIRS, AND CEILINGS

Floor Joists

With the sills set and the corner joints squared, the floor joists can be laid. However, you may prefer to proceed immediately with the walls and then the roof. If you decide to put in the joists before the walls are laid, the method shown in Figure 51 should be followed. It is quite simple. Take two 2 by 10-in. planks and nail them temporarily to the sill logs. Then lay out the points at which the joists are to be located. Measure the length of each joist separately and carefully cut them to these lengths. Next remove the planks from the sill logs and spike the joists between them, each in its proper place. Forty-penny spikes should be used for this purpose. Now set the assembled joists in place between the sills. This frame should fit tightly. Level off the frame and fasten the assembly to the sills with 40-penny spikes.

If the floor joists are laid after the walls and roof are built the method illustrated in Figure 52 is recommended. At A it can be seen that the framework is divided into two sections. This construction facilitates spiking the ends of the joists to the long members in the restricted working area provided by the interior of the cabin. One is fastened with spikes to the right-hand sill log, the other to the left-hand sill. The joints are supported at the center upon a log or concrete support running down the middle of the cabin as shown at B. The ends of the joists should be spiked together where they meet at the center. It goes without saying that any irregularities or bumps on the sill logs must be carefully leveled off as the carrying power of the floor depends upon how well the side planks and sills are fastened together. Joists should be spaced about 16 in. to centers.

If you are building your cabin in true backwoods style, you will use logs for floor joists. The sill logs are notched and the joists set in the notches as shown in Figure 53. Now the tops of the logs must be leveled so that the floor will be level. Since logs differ in dimensions, it would be best to lay the joists and spike them in place before hewing off. A long straight board and a level will have to be used for this purpose. If 2-in. plank flooring or a double floor is laid, the joists can be located from 18 to 24 in. apart. A 12-ft. span or more requires a supporting sill through the center as shown in Figure 52.

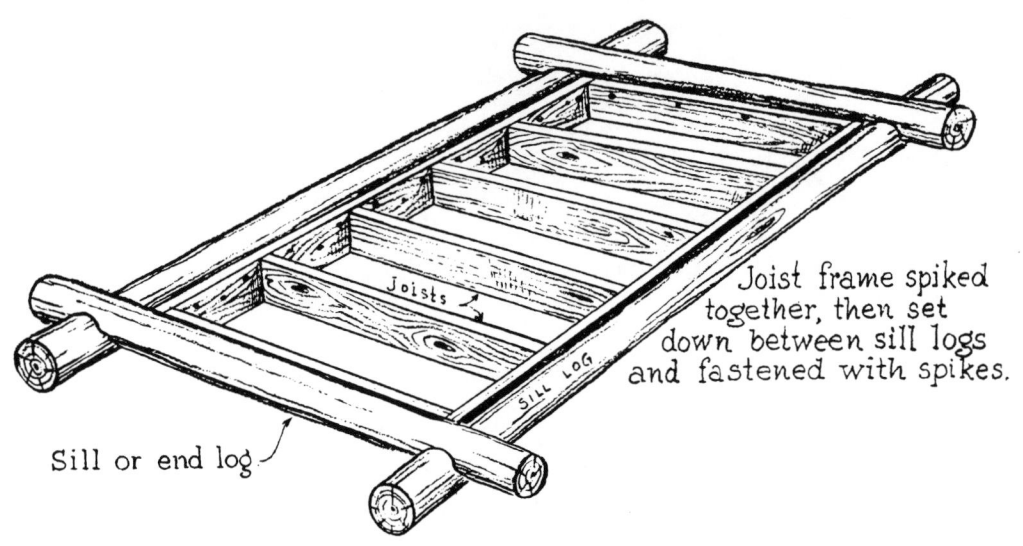

Fig. 51. Method of setting floor joists before walls are built.

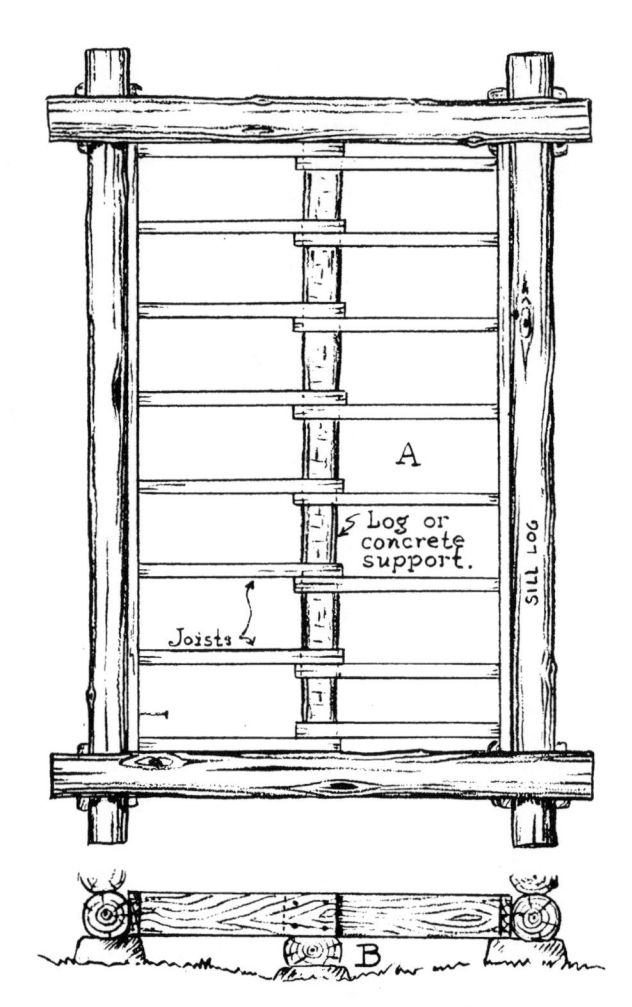

Fig. 52. Method of setting joists after walls and roof are up.

[58]

Fig. 53. Setting log joist into sill log.

Fig. 54. Floor construction.

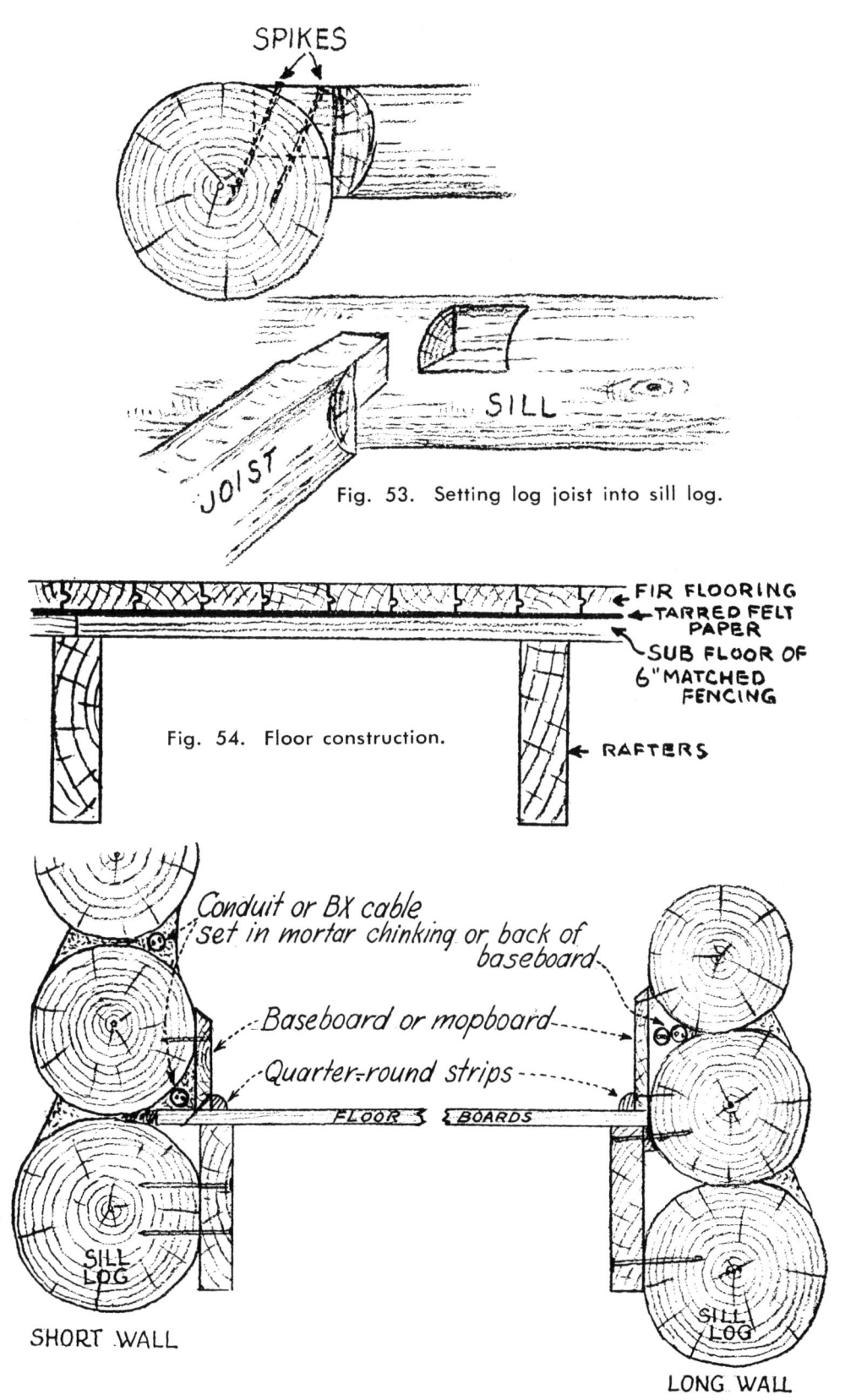

Fig. 55. Details of floor finishing around edges. Electric wiring and small water pipes can be concealed as shown. Electric outlets can be set into the mopboards.

[59]

A well-insulated ceiling sealed along the edges.

Floors

The floors should not be laid until the cabin has been chinked and the windows and doors hung. Since it is very unlikely that your cabin will have a basement, special care should be taken to build a floor that will be dry and sturdy. The ultimate in economy for a small summer cabin is a floor of 3-in., matched, yellow pine. This can be stained and waxed with excellent results. A good grade of fir porch flooring would be still better and more serviceable. An ideal type of floor construction is shown in Figure 54. Laid first is a subfloor of matched flooring of any kind or even 6-in. matched fencing. Over this a layer of good, tarred felt paper is placed. Then the floor of fir, yellow pine, or oak is laid with the boards running in the opposite direction of those of the subfloor.

Perhaps you prefer a floor made of 2-in. planks. They should be tongued and grooved and for best appearance they should measure from 8 to 12 in. in width. To prevent warping due to dampness, the bottom and edges of the planks should be oiled before they are laid and they should be fastened with heavy screws. This, of course, means work but it will be well worth the effort. For the screws, first drill a hole halfway through the plank slightly larger than the head to provide ample room for the screwdriver to turn. Then drill a lead hole slightly larger than the shank. The planks will pull down tightly. Plug the holes with dowels and cut them off flush. All the floor boards must be even before finishing is begun.

Figure 55 shows how mopboards and quarter-round molding are set around the floor.

Finishing

A good preparation for finishing a cabin is a mixture of 1 part turpentine and 3 parts boiled linseed oil to which is added a small amount of maple or walnut oil stain. It is applied liberally with a brush and after being allowed to soak for a while it is wiped off. When the first coat has dried, another thin coat is put on and permitted to dry. The floor then is given a coat or two of nonrubbing wax. If this is done about twice a year the floor will be kept in good condition. Do not varnish cabin floors and walls. If you must varnish the walls, use a flat varnish.

The same 3 to 1 mixture can be used for logs, windows, sashes, and frames. All woodwork, of course, must be cleaned before oiling. Incidentally the floor will look better if it is slightly darker than the rest of the woodwork. You can, of course, use your judgment in this matter.

Stairs

If you need a stairway for access to a second floor or a loft, it should be made of the same material as the rest of the cabin. Slabs or half logs can

Fig. 56. A single stairs made with a half log for a stringer and slots for treads.

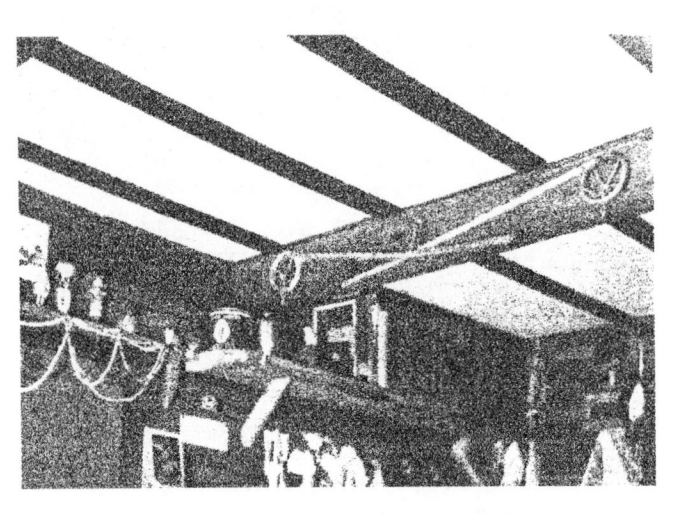

The insulating board is nailed to a ceiling of matched fencing. Note the wide battens.

be used as shown in Figure 56. It may be necessary to build the stairs steeper than shown here and perhaps a sapling rail may be required. The back of the stairway can be closed up and cupboards can be built beneath it.

Ceilings

In the small cabin a ceiling usually can be dispensed with, the roof itself forming the ceiling. If the cabin is to be used in winter, the roof should be insulated with any one of the good insulating wallboards. This can be cut to fit between the rafters or nailed over the rafters to form an air space. Painted a light color, such a ceiling will brighten the room or rooms immensely.

If the ceiling is of matched lumber, for additional insulation insulating board can be nailed against the ceiling between the joists. This will pay good dividends in cold weather and will add to your comfort during hot weather. The above photograph illustrates this treatment.

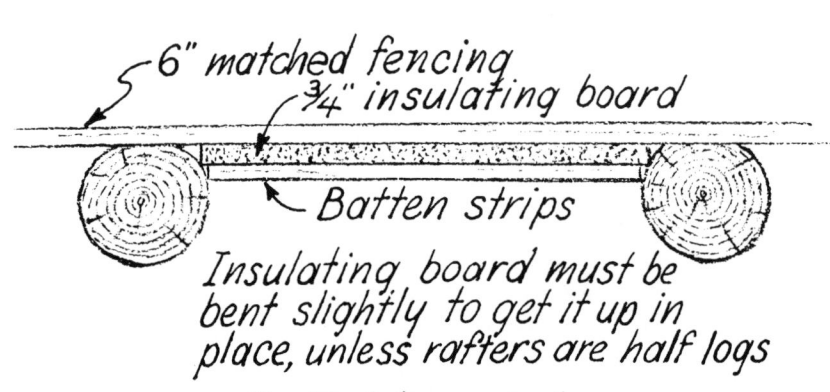

Fig. 57. Ceiling construction.

Instead of laying a double floor as is usually the case in frame houses, insulating board can be nailed between the rafters as shown in Figure 57. The photograph on page 60 shows a ceiling of insulating board in one part of my cabin. The roof was made of old lumber with heavy asphalt building paper for insulation and heavy, slate-covered, asphalt, strip shingles. This was not sufficient to hold the heat in the wintertime, so a ceiling was built as shown in the photograph. It was made of ¾-in. celotex and to gain height it was laid up against the rafters to a distance of 4 ft.

If you like icicles, don't insulate your ceiling and roof.

Chapter 9

PARTITIONS, ADDITIONS, AND PORCHES

Partitions

If there are to be log partitions or additional rooms in the form of wings, all walls are put up at the same time. Of course, if lumber or plaster is to be used, the procedure will be different. In the latter case the partitions would be built later.

Partitions can be notched as shown in Figure 58 or the logs may project as they do at the corners. Projecting ends are sometimes more picturesque. If the ends of the logs are chopped and staggered at the corners, the ends of partition logs should also be prepared in this manner. When building out a wing, it is best to dovetail the inside corners.

At this point I would like to insert an important note about partitions in larger cabins. Logs at their very best do not reflect much light. It is advisable, therefore, that you attempt to compensate for their poor light reflecting qualities. Now a light-colored plaster partition in a cabin will reflect the light from the windows and will brighten an otherwise dark room considerably. Such a wall will not detract from the appearance of rustic simplicity that you have in mind. The cabin shown in the photograph on page 14 had a plastered wall partition. This cabin, incidentally, was built in southern Wisconsin when Indians were still to be seen about the countryside. It was made of square-hewn logs with dovetail corners. The roof, which was covered with white-oak shakes, was doing good service as late as 1918. A band of Seneca Indians on the way from Green Bay to Muskego lakes stopped to watch the men who were doing the shingling. The doors of the cabin were of 2 by 6-in. matched fencing with battens on the inside.

Additions

If you have only one or two helpers, you will have more than enough work to build a one-room cabin during a single vacation season. You can always enlarge it. Even if your needs call for a more elaborate structure, it might be a good idea not to try to do the entire job in one fell swoop. In this way you will certainly enjoy the work much more and you will very likely do a better job.

For additions, of course, piers, or if you desire them, foundation walls

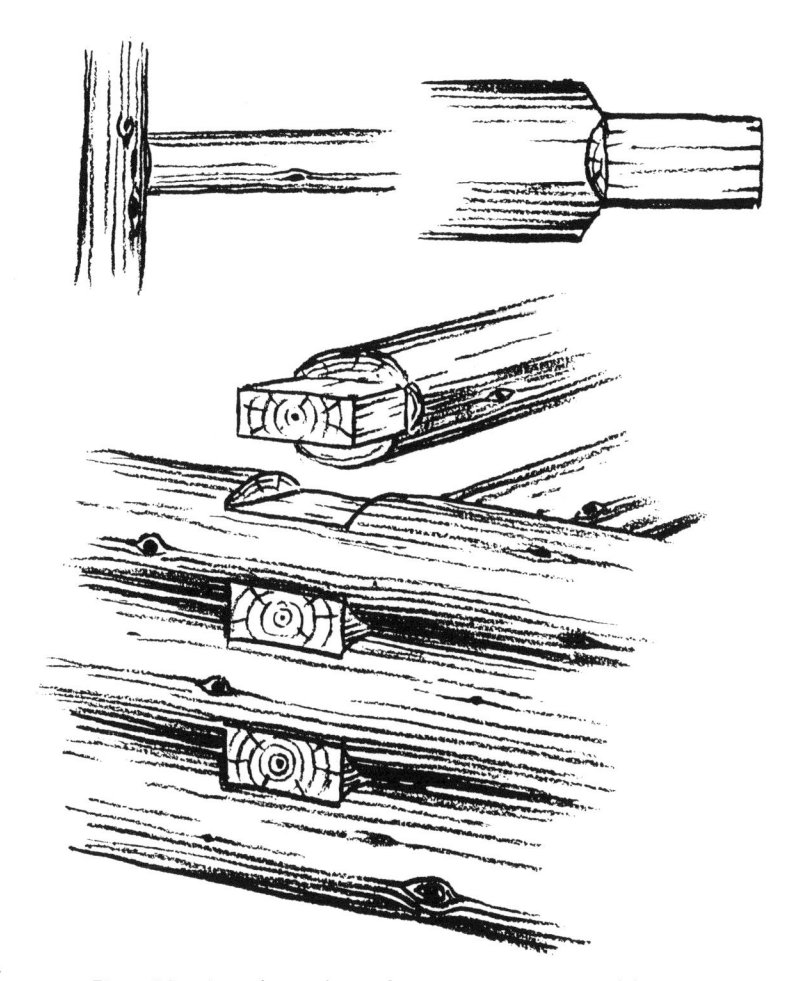

Fig. 58. Notching logs for partitions or additions.

Fig. 59. Mortise cut for partition.

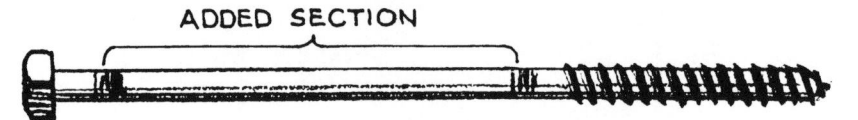

Fig. 60. Lag screw elongated by welding.

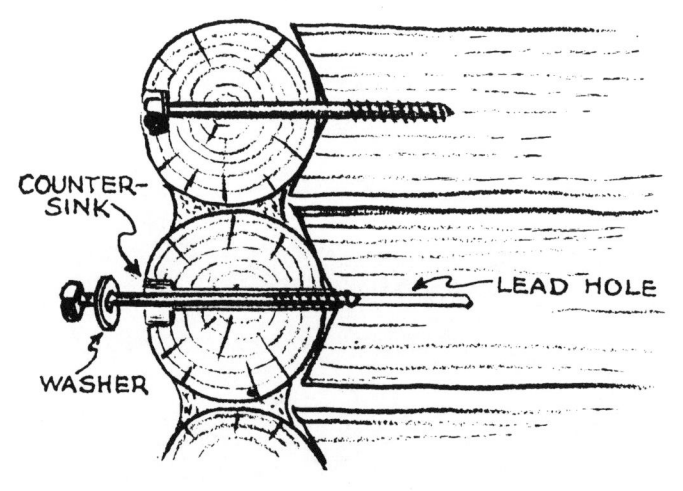

Fig. 61. New logs fastened to wall of same size logs.

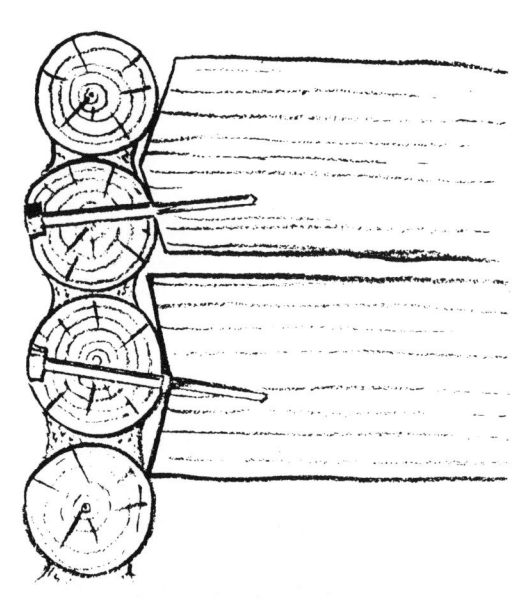

Fig. 62. Large logs fastened to wall of smaller logs.

[66]

Corner with new logs joining old logs.

or a basement, are required. They are constructed in the same manner as described previously.

Joining the addition to the cabin proper requires a little ingenuity at times. The neatest method is to tie the logs into the walls of the cabin, provided they are of the same diameter of the original ones, as shown in Figure 58. First the chinking is removed and then the mortise is cut. The upper half of the opening between the logs can be chiseled out and then the lower half can be sawed and completed with a chisel (Fig. 59). When chiseling, be careful not to loosen the chinking plaster. If the logs are small, all of the sawing can be done with a large keyhole saw. The use of this tool takes time but it is efficient.

A simpler method is to shape the ends of the new logs to conform to the sides of the old logs and fasten them with long lag screws as shown in Figure 61. These fasteners are rather scarce because they are seldom used and therefore are not often stocked in hardware stores. If you cannot buy screws of sufficient length, have a blacksmith weld pieces from 4 to 6 in. long to regular 6-in. lag screws (Fig. 60). To fasten the cedar logs to the old tamarack logs of the cabin shown in the photograph above and

Figure 62, I had to elongate the lag screws in this manner. Each log is fastened as it is laid up. A loose-fitting hole is bored through the old log and a pilot hole into the end of the new log. The holes in the old log can be countersunk to allow for a washer and the head of the lag screw. Then they are plugged with plastic wood and no one will be the wiser. The ends of the new logs can be shaped to fit with an ax or saw. The latter is much faster.

When the logs are of a different size, you will encounter a little more difficulty in obtaining a good fit. However, results will be satisfactory if the work is done as shown in Figure 62. Plaster will take care of any irregularities. As pointed out elsewhere, it is well to drive a few old nails across the larger gaps to anchor the plaster or mortar. However, drive in the nails far enough so that they will be covered.

It is not unlikely that you will need an outside door in the addition. It can be made as explained elsewhere, but it may be to your advantage to construct the door as shown in Figure 63. The ends of logs of the original unit are sawed off straight and one side of the door frame is

Fig. 63. Door frame of new section set against log ends of first section.

Door at junction of old section and addition.

set against them. Notice how the sill log is spliced to the old sill log. This method was used for an addition to my cabin. The sketch shows the details and the photograph above shows how it looked when finished.

It might be mentioned here that all the tricks and short cuts possible in log-cabin construction could not be numbered, much less described and illustrated. Hence, this work will provide ample opportunity to display your resourcefulness. I am showing some typical problems and am explaining how they were solved. With a little ingenuity and common sense any obstacle can be surmounted. Often some difficulty will call for much thought and will entail a great deal of argumentation, but then that is half the fun of building a log cabin.

Lean-tos

A lean-to is commonly used as a kitchen, woodshed, tool or work shed, or even a bedroom. It can be built of rough-sawed lumber or slabs and

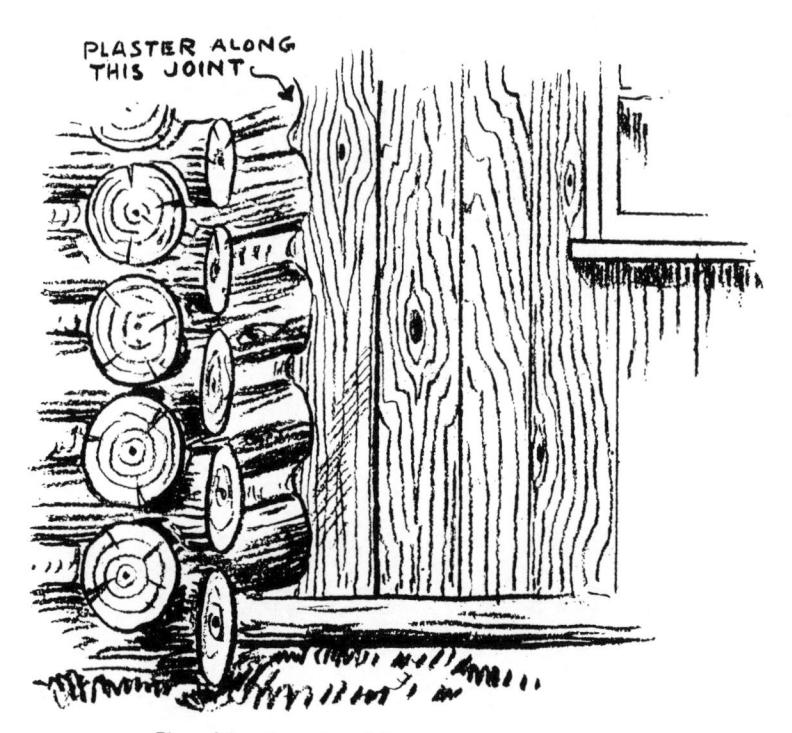

Fig. 64. Boards of lean-to cut to fit logs.

Lean-to made of logs.

can be made to harmonize with the cabin proper. The boards should be of different widths to look interesting. Batten strips, 1½ in. wide, can be nailed on the outside over the cracks. If matched lumber is used, the outside can be covered with cedar shingles. I used old barn boards for a small kitchen lean-to, but to keep out the cold in winter I covered it with a layer of building paper and shingles. The boards on such an addition should run up and down and the board next to the log wall must be cut out (Fig. 64).

Porches

Porches are designed and built for a number of purposes, some of them entirely practical, others less so. As a general rule they are constructed to

Fig. 65. Simple porch construction.

protect the doorway from rain and snow, or to provide a dry storage place for firewood. They are made larger to provide an outside, partially sheltered place for lunches and meals. Elaborate, screened porches are sometimes seen, but they more properly belong to the discussion of additions.

The photograph on page 18 shows a porch built several years ago of tamarack saplings which were plentiful at the time. This has been replaced by a new one made of cedar logs, very plain, as you can see by the photograph below, but much more substantial.

It is best to set rafters for porch roofs up and down, running parallel with the cabin (Fig. 65). The roof itself will very likely have little pitch. Hence it should be covered with a good grade of tar paper and cement rather than shingles. No rain will drive underneath this.

Porch.

Chapter 10

FIXTURES AND FIREPLACE EQUIPMENT

After the essentials of your cabin have been taken care of and the hard work is over, you will probably feel like coasting awhile. But you won't remain idle long. Soon you will have the urge to do something to make the place just a bit more pleasant and comfortable. From now on there will be a multitude of little things to be taken care of, but each job will be more fun than the previous one.

Door Latches and Locks

Of course, you will have a good tumbler lock on each door. Although these locks are modern, they are very essential. But you can make latches of hardwood like those shown in Figures 66 and 67 that will be ornamental as well as useful. The one is a sliding latch and the other a lift latch. They are placed on the inside of the door and are operated from the outside by means of either a latch string or knob. A slot must be cut in the door for the knob. For the type of latch in Figure 66 the slot is horizontal; for the one in Figure 67 it is in the form of a short arc. The wedge hanging from the nail in Figure 67 is inserted in the opening of the verticle U piece above the latch to lock the door from the inside. This latch will also lock the door automatically if the catch is smooth. A piece of brass or tin tacked on the slope of the catch will allow the latch to slide easily.

Perhaps you like wrought-iron latches and hinges. These can be purchased at hardware stores that handle building materials. The common fault, however, that I find in wrought-iron trimmings is that they are too elaborate. Remember, the pioneers had very little time and less iron. They made their hardware sturdy and simple. Wrought-iron latches (Fig. 68) can be beautiful in their simplicity and will last as long as your log cabin.

Hinges

Hinges can be forged out of heavy sheet iron or strap iron if you like to do such work. A small portable forge and anvil are very practical additions to your list of building equipment. The straps also can be cut out of sheet iron with a cold chisel and a few hammer marks can be made for effect. The straps can be put on after the ordinary hinges as shown in Figure 69.

Fig. 66. Sliding latch.

Fig. 67. Lifting latch.

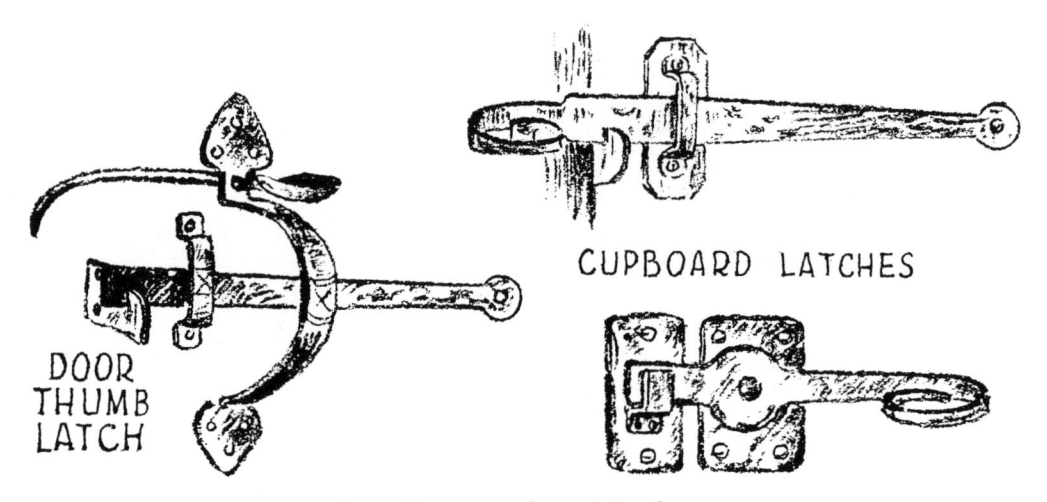

DOOR THUMB LATCH

CUPBOARD LATCHES

Fig. 68. Wrought-iron latches.

WROUGHT-IRON STRAP HINGE

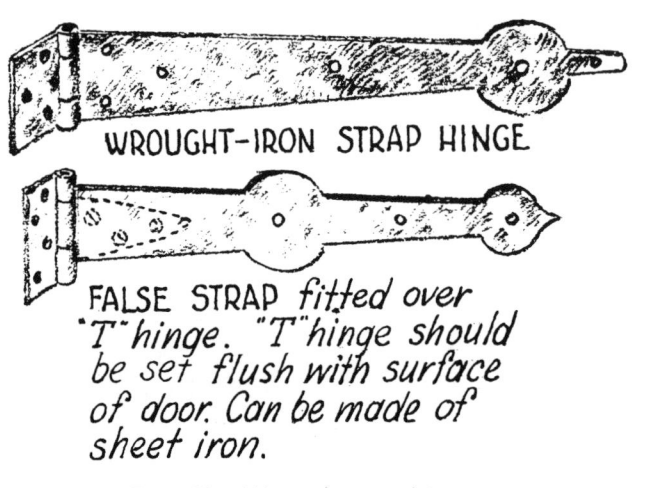

FALSE STRAP *fitted over "T" hinge. "T" hinge should be set flush with surface of door. Can be made of sheet iron.*

Fig. 69. Wrought-iron hinges.

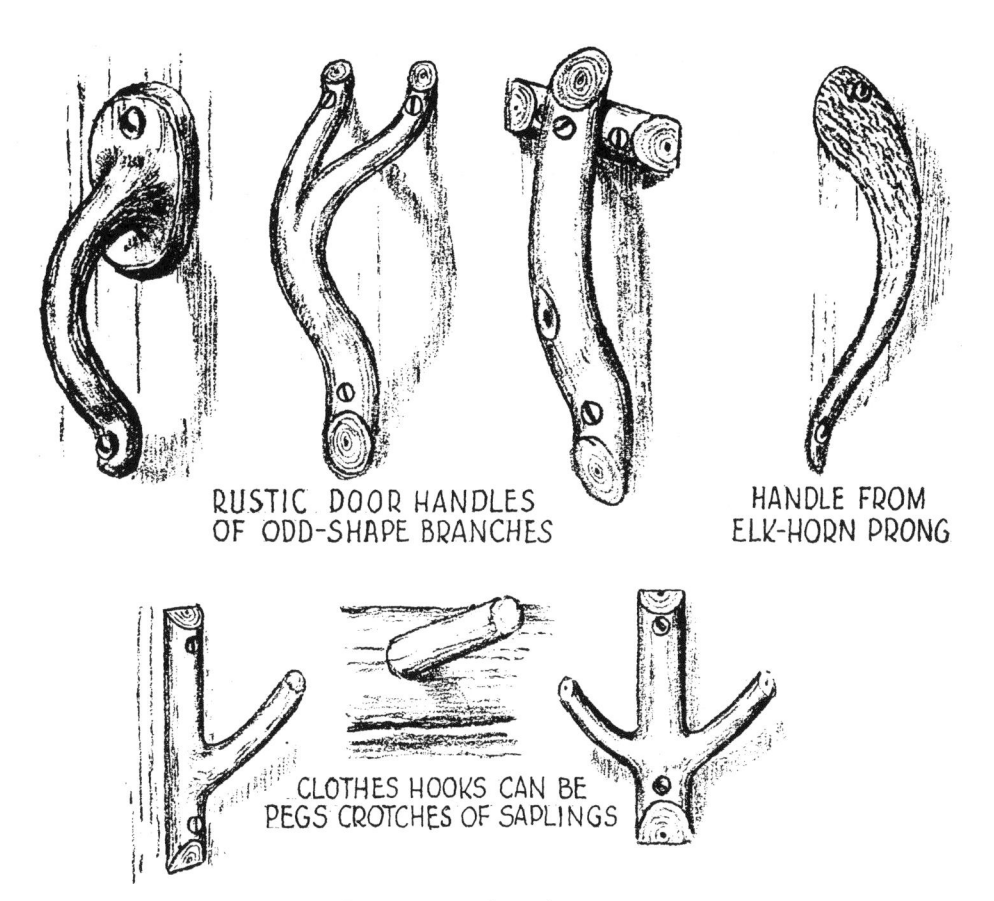

Fig. 70. Door and cupboard handles.

Door and Cupboard Handles

Handles for doors and cupboards also should be of a rustic type. Oddly shaped pieces with a natural curve are often used. Odd growths usable for this purpose can be found in the woods without too much difficulty if one is on the lookout for them. Deer and elk horn also make fine door handles (Fig. 70).

Fireplace Equipment

The early pioneers did all of their cooking over an open fire. From their fireplace equipment you can get many ideas for appointing your hearth and fireplace in a very effective manner.

Starting with andirons, you have a large choice ranging from two pieces of rail to wrought-iron firedogs (Fig. 71). The last mentioned need not be fancy, highly polished pieces of modern design; they should be the type that a country blacksmith could make out of old wagon tires.

Of equal importance is a set of fire irons. This set will include first of all a good poker with a hook on it for turning logs. Next you will need a pair of tongs to pick up hot coals and burning fragments that

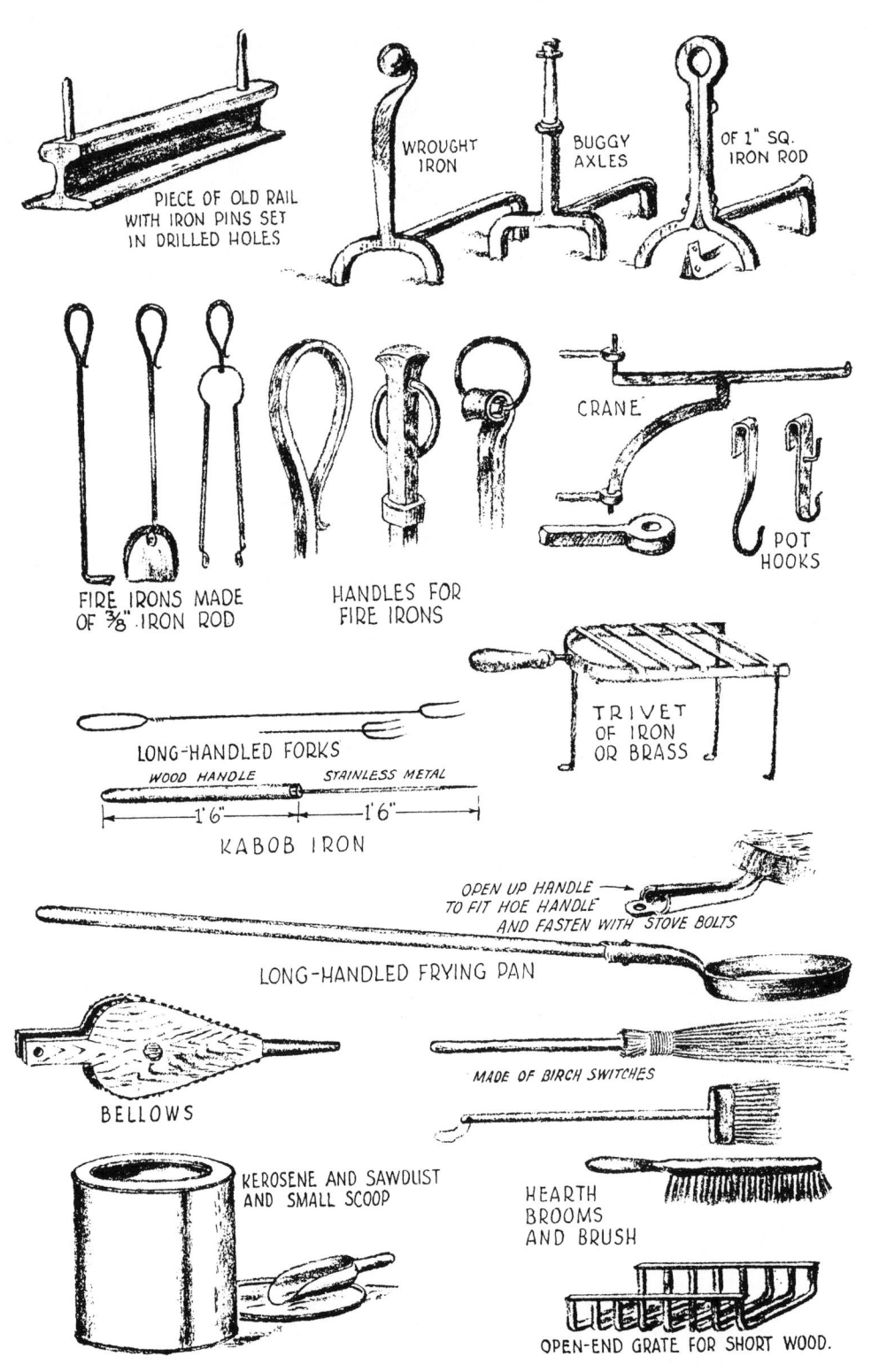

Fig. 71. Fireplace equipment.

fall off of the andirons. The third piece will be a shovel for removing the ashes.

From the crane shown in the illustration you can suspend an iron kettle and perhaps two or three pot hooks of different lengths. You might also try to find a couple of iron kettles for atmosphere.

If you are going to use your fireplace for cooking, and I know that you eventually will, there is nothing so handy as a long-handled frying pan and a long-handled broiler. There are two of each in my cabin and we would not know how to prepare a fireplace meal without them. Broilers of this kind can be purchased, but the frying-pan handle you will have to supply yourself. I once used an old hoe handle for an exceptionally large pan. Make the handle long enough, at least 4 ft., and 5 ft. is even better. It can be fastened by means of stove bolts or rivets. But don't try to fasten a long handle to a cast-iron pan. Use a stamped sheet-iron pan for this purpose. It will be a real pleasure to use this over an open fire both indoors and outdoors.

A trivet will be found very handy when cooking over an open grate. Dishes or a frying pan can be set on it.

Then make a dozen long-handled forks for roasting weiners. You may prefer kabob sticks like the one shown in the drawing. Green willow sticks can be used, but there is no danger that the metal type will burn.

Bellows are both decorative and useful. And while I am on the subject, I would like to say that the best fire starter that I know of is sawdust soaked with kerosene. It should be stored in a tight can. A handful of this material with some small wood placed over it will get a fire going in short order. This is not a genuine backwoods method of starting a fire, I suppose, but no one will complain about it when the results are seen, especially the one delegated to do the job on a cold morning.

A wood basket I hardly need mention. You will soon learn that one is very essential. You can either buy or make it yourself without great difficulty.

Two more important items should be mentioned. One is a fireplace screen. A good fire of oak, ash, or maple will seldom throw sparks into the room, but softwoods such as pine, hemlock, poplar, and basswood will. Therefore a wire screen that will cover the entire opening of the fireplace is essential. You will also find a brush or broom a handy article to have leaning against the fireplace.

Chapter 11

LIGHTING AND HEATING

Lighting

In my cabin I ran the gamut of lighting from candles to electric fixtures. We had to install electricity for practical reasons in spite of the coziness of candle and lamp light, which is used now only for very special occasions. A word about the history of my cabin will give a good picture of the evolution of lighting systems in such a dwelling.

My home is located on the outskirts of a small town on a plot of land that extends from a main highway several hundred feet to a brook. Toward the rear the property is rather heavily wooded and it is here that the log cabin was erected, for building in the northwoods or elsewhere at that time was not possible as far as I was concerned. The cabin was intended primarily for use as a work and tool house. There were benches for woodwork and iron work and in one corner a forge and anvil (see the photograph on page 79). Heat was supplied only by the fireplace. It was a swell place for friendly gatherings and we thoroughly enjoyed working there, making wrought-iron fixtures, rustic furniture, and so on. One gasoline lantern was used, to which we added a large tin reflecting shade to throw the light down on the work. It provided more than enough illumination except when it ran out of gasoline and this occurred usually when the light was needed most.

We then decided to convert the cabin into a gift shop. Some remodeling was required. A center partition of knotty pine was put in. Shelves were built on the partition and along the walls. We discovered that in order to display lighting fixtures and wrought-iron and other semirustic lamps the cabin would have to be wired. BX cable was used for this purpose and was run between the logs as shown in Figure 55.

The gift shop was a success, but the family decided to use the cabin as sort of a summer home. We lived in it for a few weeks every spring while our garden was being prepared and planted. It was fun. During the evenings I made rustic lamps and fixtures to dress up the cabin. These lamps, of course, were electrified and the wiring was concealed. They provided adequate light for reading and working.

Recently my cabin has been converted into a combination museum and workshop. It has been enlarged and remodeled. The rooms have ivory celotex ceilings. There are two flush lights in the ceiling of the larger room and four Indian katcina lamps on the walls. This arrangement provides a much better distribution of light than the old gasoline lamp, not to mention a more pleasant atmosphere. Now we have light whenever and wherever we need it. Candlelight we use on occasion and often we do without light entirely and sit before a bright, crackling fire of cedar or poplar logs and go back a hundred years.

Unless you are going modern, there will be no wide concrete walks

Author at forge and anvil used for wrought-iron work.

around your cabin and leading to it. It is more than likely that you will have flagstone or gravel walks. While these can be made very firm they are never as smooth as concrete. Then, too, the nights will be dark and there will be many trees around and about — hence the need for good porch and yard light. You can make the fixtures yourself, but be sure that they illuminate the grounds and do not blind. Rustic lamps strategically placed are therefore very practical and will enhance the beauty of your place.

In planning your lights and lighting system you will have a fine opportunity to express your individuality. It is hardly possible to make specific recommendations that would be equally acceptable to the varying tastes of individual builders. In my cabin the Indian motif is pronounced. The walls are decorated with Indian clothing, pipes, tomtoms, and eagle feathers. Whatever you do, keep your cabin rustic.

Coal and wood stove.

Wood-burning stove made of 50-gallon oil drum.

Heating

I suppose that when everything is said and done, adequate heating is the most important requirement in a cabin that is to be used in cold weather. In moderate temperature, a fireplace is able to keep a cabin comfortably warm. But a fireplace alone will not suffice in severe cold unless it is of the Heatolator type, which has been discussed already. An ideal combination is a fireplace and some kind of stove. Thus the stove will supply ample heat and the fireplace will draw the cold air from the floor and carry it up the chimney. The latter, of course, will throw out a good amount of heat, especially after it has been in operation for about two hours and the stones and bricks are heated through.

For efficiency, economy, and atmosphere, the combination stove shown in the photograph to the left on this page cannot be surpassed. It burns wood and coal. A fire can be kept going for about twelve hours and the room will stay warm. It will operate at about a quarter of the cost of an oil stove.

The other stove shown above was made from a 40-gal. oil drum. Firebricks 1 in. thick were laid on the bottom of the drum and part way up the sides to retain the heat. Such a stove can be made easily by anyone who is handy with tools. This quick-heating stove will warm a 16 by 28-ft. room within an hour during subzero weather. A fire can be kept going in it overnight if a couple of green chunks of wood are tossed into it on retiring. Coal cannot be used because there is no grate.

Of course, other types of wood stoves will also serve well in cold weather. For example there is the wood-burning cooking and baking oven which was common a few years back. A sheet-iron stove like the one in Figure 72 is quick-heating, but like all wood stoves it requires constant attention. However, in the experience of the author, the combination wood and coal stove discussed above will supply ample heat at all times with a minimum of attention and will add rather than detract from the appearance of the cabin.

Some people may prefer an oil stove, with which the author also has experimented. An oil stove, however, will not harmonize with the rest of the interior of the cabin as well as a good wood stove.

Fig. 72. Airtight stove.

Chapter 12

RECONDITIONING OLD LOG CABINS

If you have come into possession of an old log cabin or if your own cabin is in need of repair, you probably will like a few suggestions for reconditioning it. The typical city home can be fixed readily with paint or wallpaper or both. A log cabin, however, is different in this respect and may require improvements that are a bit more difficult to make.

One of the most common defects in old cabins is loose chinking. This, of course, must be removed completely and a little trouble will be encountered at times.

Next, the logs must be cleaned. If they are pealed, they will have become darkened with age and will need scraping. The logs can be shaved with an ordinary short-handled floor scraper, provided they are smooth, that is, without too many knots. There are several different types of floor scrapers on the market (Fig. 73); the type of scraper used by cabinet-makers will also work. Some have reversable blades, and others, double blades. A long-handled scraper, however, is the best. These tools must be sharp and must be kept in that condition for satisfactory results. After the loose chinking has been removed, the logs can readily be prepared to look new and fresh without too much difficulty.

If the bark is still on the logs the problem is altogether different. Now the first unit of my cabin was made of unpeeled tamarack. Only the loose outer bark had been scraped off. The logs looked very excellent at the time. The reddish browns and purples gave the walls a beautiful color. Soon, however, large black ants and other borers began to inhabit our elegant walls and eventually the bark had to be removed. For this I made scrapers of old files about 1½ in. wide. The ends were heated and flattened to a sharp edge and then bent as shown in Figure 73. With a scraper of this kind and a good pair of arms and wrists, in one motion you can remove bark and from ¼ to ⅜ in. of sapwood in which the bugs like to bore. If the tool is held at the correct angle, a cutting action can be effected which will produce a much smoother finish than scraping, but the scraper must be sharpened every so often.

After the bark has been removed, brush off the dusk and rechink as necessary. For applying the mortar, use a small trowel and a hawk, as shown in Figure 74. I used a small molders' tool employed for finishing sand molds and have not found anything superior to it for a partially

FLOOR & CABINET SCRAPERS **SCRAPER FROM OLD FILE**

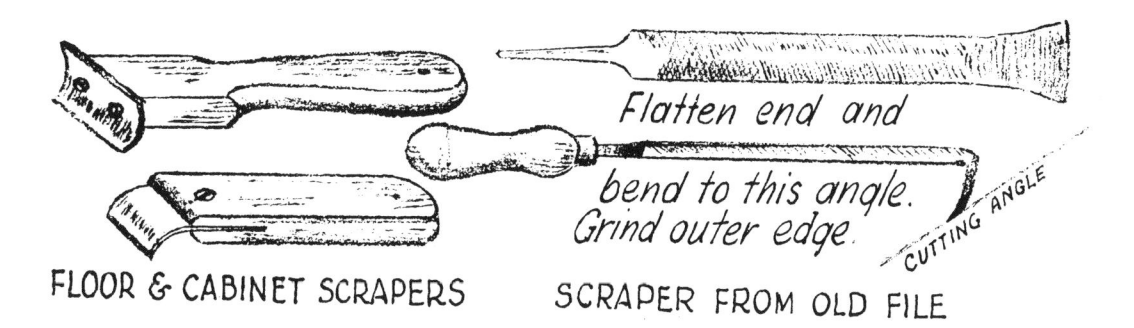

Flatten end and bend to this angle. Grind outer edge. CUTTING ANGLE

Fig. 73. Scrapers.

chinked wall. When a section of about 3 ft. is completed, go over the plaster with a 4-in. wet paint brush. For this operation a brush was kept on hand in a pan of water. Both old and new plaster was given this treatment with the result that you see in the photograph. Trowel marks are effective in new chinking but not for patches in old mortar.

If the logs have been scraped clean, they need only be oiled. The walls will be very light and will look like new. The outside walls can also be scraped and rechinked but need not be oiled.

Floors

If old floors are not too badly worn, they can be sanded with a power floor sander. A machine of this type can be rented. As a rule, however, it is better to lay new flooring crosswise. To lay linoleum over a rough floor is a waste of time and money.

Removing bark with bent-file scraper.

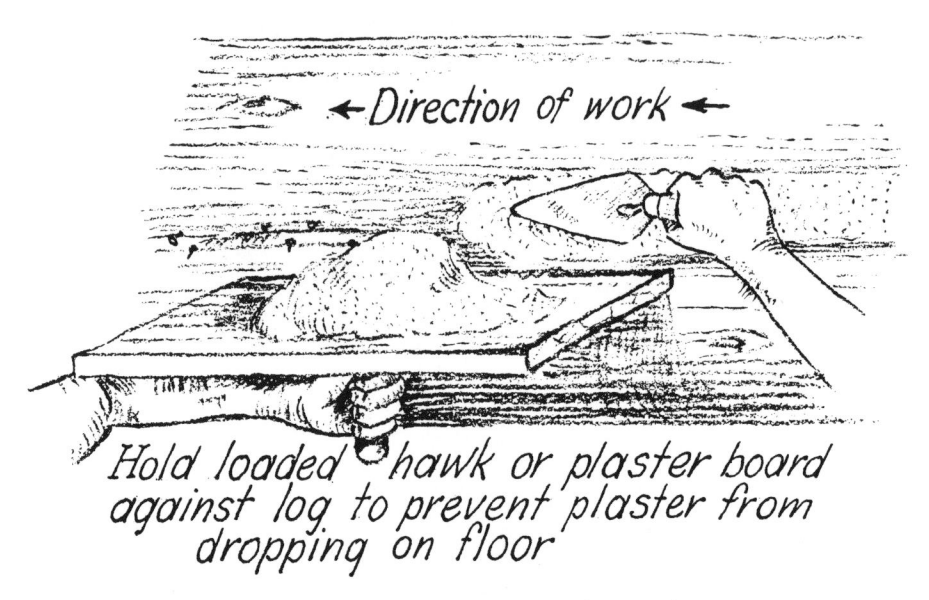

Fig. 74. Small trowel and hawk used for applying mortar.

Ceilings

For a new ceiling any one of the many different kinds of insulating board can be nailed over the old one. On the other hand, it may be necessary to put up an entirely new ceiling. The openings can be filled with wood mortar where the insulating board meets the logs, and large battens can be used to cover the joints between the sections.

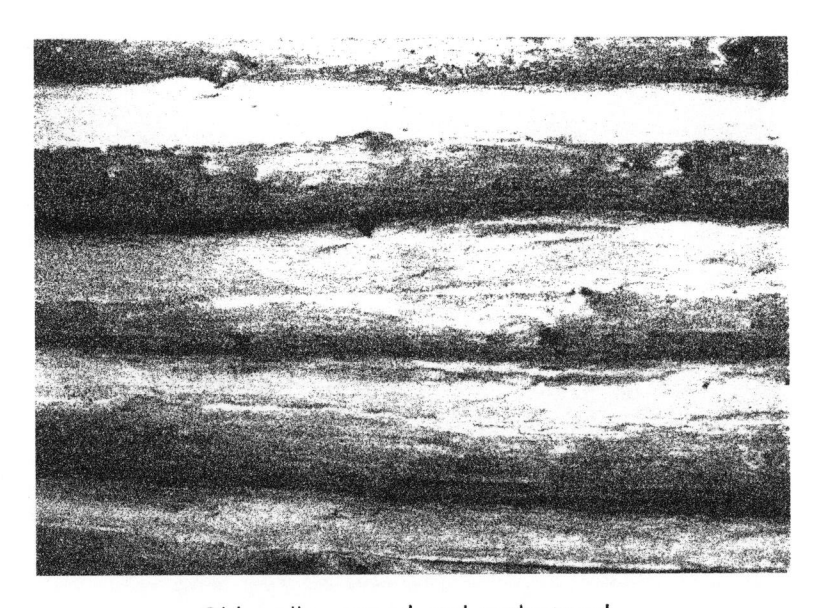

Old walls scraped and replastered.

Chapter 13

OUTDOOR FIREPLACES

Though the interior of your cabin may be beautiful and comfortable, there will be many times during the summer months that you will want to eat outdoors, the mosquitoes permitting. It is more than likely, therefore, that you will want some kind of outdoor fireplace on your grounds. Everyone who cooks outdoors has his pet theory concerning outdoor fireplaces. Let us consider a few types here and you can then determine which one will suit your needs best.

The first question that I ask a person desiring information on outdoor fireplaces is: For what purpose are you going to use it? Possibly you want it to roast weiners or to prepare hamburgers, steaks, corn, or bean-hole beans. There are those, too, who like to prepare an entire meal on an outdoor fireplace. A few points, therefore, should be taken into consideration before you build. A little planning will be well worth the satisfaction of having a well-constructed and efficient fireplace. Of course, if you are a camp cook and a master of all of the tricks of camp cooking, and in addition don't mind blackened pots and pans, you may not even need a fireplace.

During the past few years, very beautiful outdoor fireplaces of the chimney type have been built both in parks and on private grounds. The typical fireplace of this kind is made of the same stone used for the house, has pleasing proportions, and is located at some choice point on the property. Chimney fireplaces are rarely passed without being noticed and admired. However, you probably will not be looking for something quite so elaborate, and they do have one drawback. The outside of the chimney nearest the fire is inclined to become blacker than the flue. Why? I'll answer this question with a question. Why should the smoke seek its way over to the chimney when there is nothing to prevent it from rising directly upward? Smoke simply will follow the line of least resistance. Thus these chimneys are ornamental rather than functional. Logically, if you wanted the chimney to work you would be required to build an outdoor stove. If smoke is to go up a chimney, every other outlet must be closed. All of this, however, is still no argument against the beauty of the chimney fireplace. Here, however, we will limit ourselves to a few basic designs of the simpler type of outdoor fireplace. I trust

A. Sectional view.

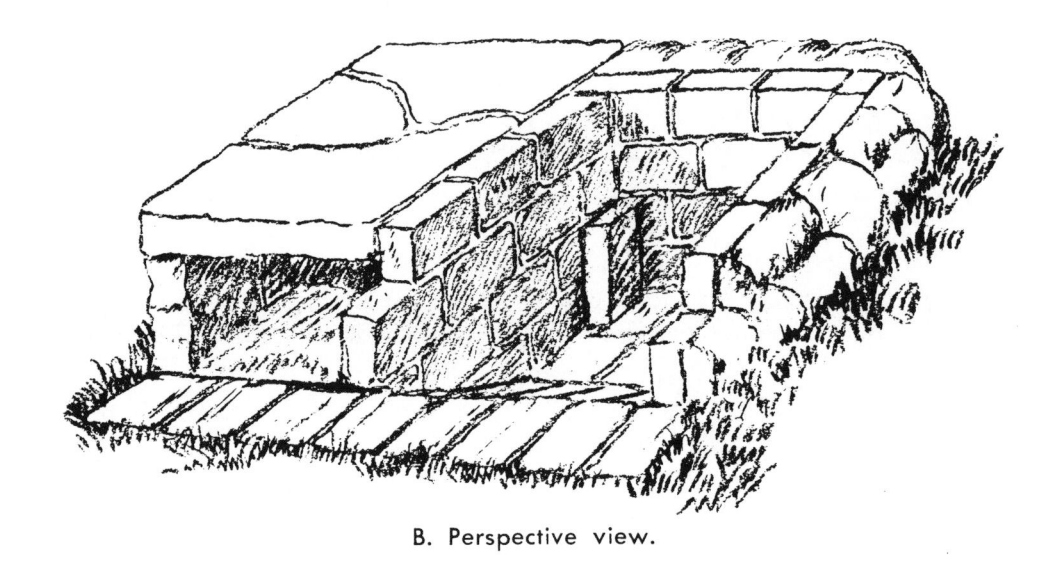

B. Perspective view.

Fig. 75. Pit fireplace.

that my experience with them will help you in planning and building one that will have all of the features you will want.

Materials

The principles governing the selection of materials for outdoor fireplaces are the same as those for indoor fireplaces. You will recall that in our discussion of the latter, you were warned about the danger of exploding stones. It was explained that while some stones will react favorably to heat, some will not; hence the advisability of using firebrick for the firepot. While my present outdoor fireplace has caused no difficulty in this regard, let me tell you of my experience with one that did. A few years ago I made a very fine fireplace in northern Michigan, where we had to do all our cooking outdoors. Fortunately I did not go to the trouble of using mortar but merely saw to it that the stones were laid up symmetrically and firmly. We then went about the not too unpleasant task of preparing our first meal. A fire was started and everything was coming along very well until the stones started to explode. It's a good joke now but then it was far from funny. We ate a cold meal that night. I have seen this same thing happen many times since and am always sceptical, therefore, when using stone in a strange locality. To play safe, line your outdoor fireplace with firebrick just as you did with the fireplace in your cabin. You will note that firebrick is shown in each drawing. I used it in my fireplace not only to insure myself against the possibility of having to build another one but also because they are easier to work with. The facing that you see in the photographs is cut limestone. Any field stone can be used around the outside, for only the firebrick lining will have to withstand very intense heat. You can also use common building brick for the exterior if no stones are available.

Pit Fireplace

The pit fireplace shown in Figure 75 is ideal for preparing bean-hole beans, roasted corn, and is very satisfactory for all other types of roasting, broiling, and frying. Built with a firebrick lining, it is easy to clean out with a rake or hoe. The ashes are simply pulled up the incline and disposed of. A shovel also can be used. Then, too, you can easily rake out the live embers to provide for a dutch oven on the hot firebrick and then shovel or push them back to cover the pot. Similarly in the pit fireplace, the embers easily can be raked right over the corn for roasting.

This fireplace has one drawback; it is rather low. On the other hand, a low fireplace is better for a camp fire than a high one. When you stop to think how people enjoy sitting around a fire at night after a good outdoor meal, a fireplace that will hold a fire is very desirable.

Figure 75A is a sectional view of a pit fireplace. The upright brick in the lower right corner is a support for the grate, the lower end of which rests on the ground in front. If this brick is set higher, you will have to use a brick in front so that the grate will be level, but then you will not have to raise the grate to put wood on the fire.

Figure 75B shows the pit fireplace in perspective. Here it can be seen clearly how the stone is mortared around the brick. At the left is a table of flat stone for pots and pans. If this is open, kindling wood can be stored here and, of course, a rather large stone will be required.

Surface Fireplace

The surface fireplace shown in Figure 76 will be found very satisfactory for general, all-round, outdoor cooking. You will notice that there are no projecting iron lugs such as are sometimes used to support the

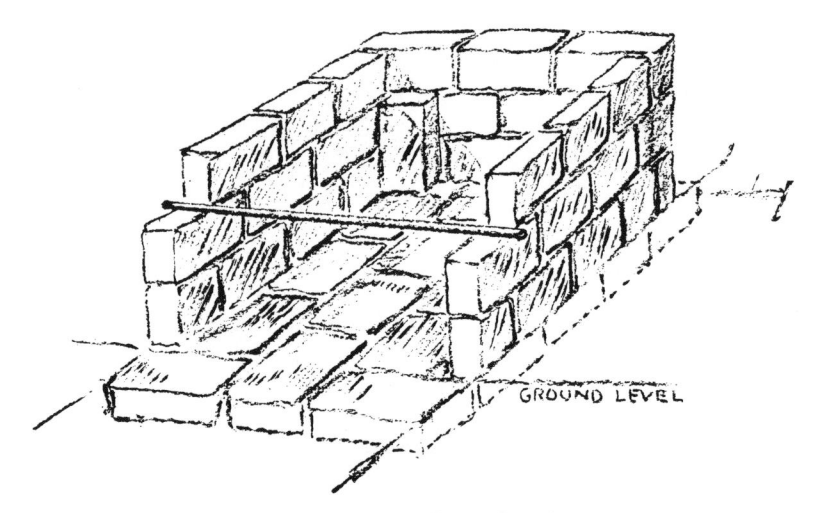

Fig. 76. Surface fireplace.

Fig. 77. Raised fireplace.

Surface fireplace.

grates nor are there any other unnecessary fixtures. The floor is set flush with the ground. Stone of any kind should be mortared around, as brick set on end would not hold. Note the brick mortared in the corner. It is level with the projecting bricks in front. A loose iron rod will support the forward end of the grate and the corner bricks will hold the other end. If the rod is loose, it can be removed for cleaning out the fireplace or starting fires.

As far as baking is concerned, with the reflector oven in the photograph on page 90 you can get some very fine results. With a good fire, you can bake a pan of biscuits in about ten minutes in this oven. At the same time you can bake corn or broil steaks on the fireplace proper. This will hurry along the preparation of the meal. I used an old window grate with bars about 1½ in. apart, which is just about right for sweet corn in husks. The corn is soaked in water from four to eight hours before roasting time. The ears are then laid on the grate close together, and if the fire is at all brisk, you can keep the upper half of the ears wet with a bundle of corn husks without putting out the fire. Then after about fifteen minutes, depending on the heat, the ears are turned and the green sides are roasted, the corn again being kept moist as described above. The sprinkling is done to prevent the corn from drying out and thus it is steamed and roasted

Reflector oven used in conjunction with a surface fireplace.

at the same time. I have not as yet had a word of complaint about corn prepared this way. But this is not intended to be a "dissertation on roast corn." So let us move on to our next fireplace.

Raised Fireplace

The fireplace shown in Figure 77 is merely an adaptation of the surface fireplace just discussed. It has the advantage, however, of being elevated and thus makes stooping less of a problem. The bricks are laid flat. Any odd field stone or common brick can be used for the base. Loose brick laid in front of the fireplace will prevent embers from rolling out in front where the cook stands. The shelf is very handy for plates and utensils. All in all, this would constitute about as fine a fireplace as any. True, it is not quite as good as the pit type for a camp fire, but if fairly large, dry logs are placed in it in tepee fashion, you can get enough of a fire for all practical purposes.

As in previous chapters, I have given you what might be termed basic helps or suggestions. No doubt you have variations in mind that will prove very practical. For example, you might want more shelf area. Whatever the case may be, don't hesitate to launch right out with your ideas. A final suggestion might be made here. It might not be a bad idea to build your outdoor fireplace as soon as you have determined where the cabin is to stand. Thus you will get a great deal of use out of it when the cabin is being built.

Chapter 14

HELP WANTED

Unless you are a superman and intend to do all the work on your log cabin by yourself, you will do well to consider the list of men whose assistance you would like to have. Perhaps friends will be willing to help you, or should I say, perhaps you are fortunate enough to know some good fellows who are willing to work. On the other hand, you may have to hire from one to three or four men if you are pressed for time. Whatever your employment situation proves to be, the following are the workers required to build a cabin.

Architect

If your cabin is going to be of a more pretentious type, you will very likely enlist the services of an architect. For the relatively simple dwelling that we have been discussing I hardly think that an architect will be required. From the instructions given herein you can plan almost any kind of small cabin by yourself. But you must use good common sense and know something about costs of and procuring material.

Ax Men

Here we do not have reference to loggers but rather to men who can handle a small hand ax. Most of the notching can be done with a hand ax. As a matter of fact there is very little chopping that requires a large ax unless the ends of the logs are to be chopped.

Adz Men

There is always a certain amount of adz work. Sometimes the smoothing out, or flattening, of logs for sills, rafters, and so on, can be done with an ax but a man who is handy with an adz can do the job a lot better and faster. A broad ax is sometimes used if the logs to be faced can be turned. An adz is also better than an ax for round notching, other things being equal.

Sawyers

You probably think that anyone can saw a log in two. You are quite correct, but only one out of a dozen can make a straight cut. And remember, as we have pointed out previously, a straight cut is very essential at door and window openings.

Carpenters

Carpenters are very good to have around to make window and door frames, to square up sills and rafters, and to lay floors. And when it comes to making doors, a fellow with carpenter experience will prove a mighty valuable asset. He also has a lot of tricks up his sleeve for roof and porch construction.

Drawknifer

This is another very important helper. The requirements of his job are long, powerful arms and ability to eye up a log and round it where necessary. Not everyone can handle a drawknife. When properly drawknifed, a log has the appearance of being freshly peeled. All peeled logs should be drawknifed if they are to be stained. Also, the inner side of old logs must be similarly shaved for staining. Log rafters can be leveled with a drawknife. Thus the drawknife proves to be a most essential tool and the drawknife man a most essential worker.

My father was a champion log sitter.

Mason and Cement Workers

Don't ever get the idea that anyone can lay up a stone fireplace. Masonry is a trade and making a real fireplace is an art. Cement workers are not so essential except that they know what to do and how to do it in the shortest possible time — and time is a big item.

Electrician

If electricity is available, you will undoubtedly make use of it. A good electrician will be very welcome especially if the conduit or BX cable is to be laid in cement or plaster. Once laid, it is there to stay. Be sure to have him install a sufficient number of base plugs where you think they will be needed most.

Plumber

You probably have had little or no experience in installing plumbing so you had better get a plumber. If your cabin is to stand idle all winter, be sure that all water pipes can be drained properly.

Log Sitter

Now we come to one of our most important helpers, the log sitter. Have you ever tried to saw a log without the help of someone to keep it from turning? Have you ever attempted to saw off the end of a log without someone to hold it to prevent splitting? Finally, have you ever tried to use an adz on a small log that was not steadied? If this has been your experience I am sure you will need no sale talk on the need for this valuable co-worker. But the log sitter is more than his occupational classification implies for he is in fact a general handy man. He can do a hundred and one things around your cabin that others might consider unimportant. He is the fellow who will give you a lift when you need it. He is on hand to toss up that missing spike, to get that odd-size piece of lumber, and so on. Perhaps he can also cook up a good meal. So don't neglect him. He will be most useful from start to finish in all phases of construction.

This completes your staff. You probably won't need the help of all of these men at the same time. And then, too, it is very likely that some of them will qualify for more than one job.

At this time I wish to thank the many friends who have helped me at this work and who have thus shared in a way in the production of this book. If I were to attempt to name them all there would be quite a list. They always were ready to lend a hand when the going was tough. Their ready wit, their willingness, their pride in doing everything right, their pleasantness made the job recreation rather than labor. Most of the fellows still drop in at the cabin to visit a moment or to spend an evening

Well worth the effort!

and I can't help thinking of the contribution each one made materially and socially. The old expression "a friend in need is a friend indeed" I suppose is a bit worn out at the cuffs but it certainly takes on fuller meaning after you have had the opportunity of working with a group of good fellows.

With wise planning, proper tools and materials, and pleasant, efficient help, building a log cabin can be a lot of fun. Moreover your efforts will be more than amply rewarded, for you will have something that will give unique enjoyment for many years to come.

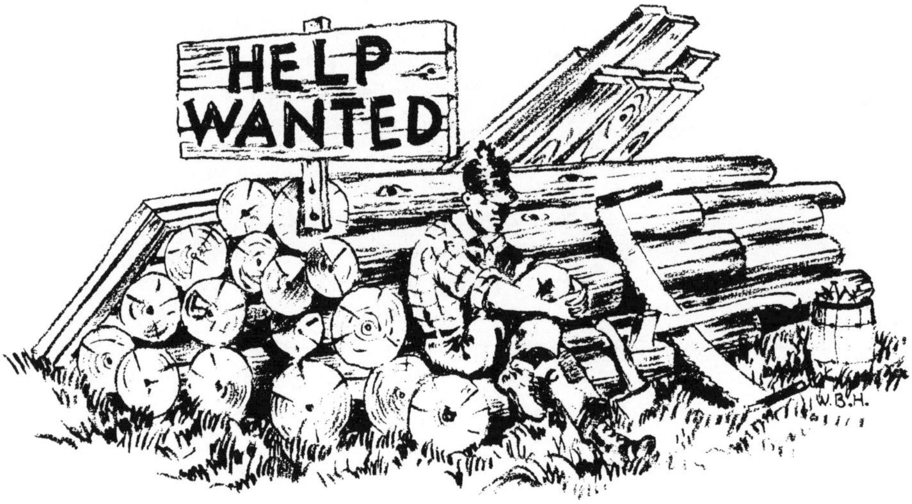
HELP
WANTED
W.B.H.

INDEX

A-and-V joint, 31
Accessibility of cabin, 14–15
Additions, 64–69
Adz, 19, 21, 92
Andirons, 75
Architect, 92
Ax
 broad, 19, 21, 92
 hand, 19, 21, 92
 large, 19, 21, 92
Ax-cut ends, 32

Balsam, 16
Band saw used for ripping logs, 40
Basement, 23–25
Bellows, 77
Broiler, long-handled (fireplace), 77
Broom (fireplace), 77
Brush (fireplace), 77

Cant hook, 19
Carborundum wheel, 21
Carpenter, 93
Cedar, 16
Ceiling, 41, 62–63
Ceiling joists, 41
Chinking, 41–45
Chisel, 19, 21
Common joint, 31–32
Crane (fireplace), 77
Crayon, marking, 21
Crosscut saw, 19
Cupboard handles, 75

Dividers, 19
Door handles, 75
Door latches, 73
Doors, 54–56
 frames, 35, 37
 openings for, 35, 37
 trim, 40
Dovetail joints, 33
Drainage, 11–12
Drawknife, 19, 21, 93
Dutch doors, 56

Eaves, 47
Electrician, 94
Emery wheel, 21
End logs, 30

File
 flat mill, 21
 triangular, 21
Finishing logs, 45–46
Fire clay, 28

Firedogs, 75
Fire irons (fireplace), 75–76
Fireplace
 equipment, 75–77
 erection, 25–29
 opening for, 36
 outdoor, *see* Outdoor fireplaces
 screen, 77
 sheet-iron unit, 27
Fire starter, 77
Flashing, 49–50
Floor, 30
Floor joists, 41, 57
Floors, 57–61
 finishing, 61
 laying, 60–61
Foundation
 piers, 22–23
 wall, 23–24
Foundations, 22–25
Froe, 19
Frying pan, long-handled (fireplace), 77

Gables, 47–49
Gouge, 19
Grindstone, 21
Guide for cutting log ends, 37

Hammer, 19
Heating (in addition to fireplace), 80–81
Hinges, 73

Ice tongs, 19

Joints, 30–35
 A-and-V, 31
 common, 31–32
 dovetail, 33
Joists
 ceiling, 41
 floor, 41

Kabobs, iron for, 77

Lean-to, 9, 69–71
Level, 19
Lighting, 78–79
Logs, 16–18
 balsam, 16
 cedar, 16
 electric-line poles, 16
 finishing, 45–46
 ordering, 17
 poplar, 16
 qualities of good, 16
 rafter, 16–17

seasoning, 17
shrinkage of, 41
sources of, 16
spruce, 16
tamarack, 16
white pine, 16
Lumber
shrinkage of, 41

Mallet, wooden, 19
Marking gauge, 32
Mason, 94
Miter-box arrangement for cutting log ends, 37
Mortar, 44
"Mud dauber," 43

Notching gauge, 19

Oakum, 44–45, 51
Orientation of cabin, 12–14
Outdoor fireplaces, 85–91
materials, 86–87
pit type, 87
raised type, 90–91
surface type, 87–90

Partitions, 64
Piers, 22–23
Plate log, 47
Plumb bob, 19
Plumber, 94
Poplar, 16
Porches, 71–72

Rafters, 47
Reconditioning old cabins, 82
ceiling, 84
floors, 83
walls, 82–83
Reflector oven, 89–90
Ridge board, 47
Roof, 47–51
Roof boards, 47
Roof patching, 50
Roof pitch, 47
Roofing cement, 50–51
Roofing material, 47, 50

Safety factor in selecting site, 15
Sanding machine, 83
Saw, 21, 92–93
Scrapers for logs, 82
Seasoning logs, 17
Second floor, 41

Septic tank, 11–12
Sharpening tools, 21
Shingles
cedar, 50
cypress, 50
wood, 47, 50
Shrinkage of logs, 41
Shutters, 56
Sill logs, 30
anchoring, 24
Site, 9–15
accessibility, 14–15
drainage, 11–12
orientation, 12–14
preparation, 22
safety, 15
water supply, 12
Sphagnum moss, 44–45
Springhouse, 12
Spruce, 16
Square, 19
Stairs, 61–62
Stone, cracking from heat, 17–18
Stoves, 80–81

Tamarack, 16
Tapeline, 21
Tar paper, 47, 50
Tools, 21
Triangular, 21
Trivet, 77

Walls, 30–46
Water supply, 12
Weather stripping, 52
Well
deep, 12
drilled, 12
driven, 12
dug, 12
Well points, 12
White pine, 16
Window spring bolts, 52
Window stop, 52
Windows
casement, 52
double-hung, 52
frames, 35, 37–40
openings for, 35, 37–40
picture, 52
tilting, 52
trim, 40
weather stripping, 52
Wood basket, 77
Wrecking bar, 19–20

Printed in Great Britain
by Amazon